"No one I know presents Jesus' lo[...] [...] more winsomely and compellingly,] with greater joy and verve, than Jolene. Her Spirit-anointed stories hold people spellbound."
   —DALE COOPER, Chaplain, Calvin College

"Jolene has an amazing gift. Her stories of hardship and hope truly connect with those in need."
   —TERRI DEBOER, TV personality, Grand Rapids, MI

"It's a shame that people in search of inspiration so often choose only those writers that are already well known, because they miss out on the fresh energy of genuine grace-givers like Jolene. If you're looking for some great stories about a great and loving God, look no further. Jolene is a genuine Red Letter Christian!"
   —DR. TONY CAMPOLO, Eastern University

"Jolene saved my life. I desperately needed to know that God loves me."
   —ALLY, who had attempted suicide

"Jolene takes you on an emotional roller coaster—laughing one minute and crying the next."
   —NECIA VANDER WALL, former youth pastor, Pathways Church, Michigan

"Jolene is real. God is using her mightily."
   —FRANKIE WUNDERINK, youth pastor, Grace Valley Church, Nevada

"I learned from Jolene what it means to hunger and thirst after God, and what a passionate and life-giving relationship with Abba looks, sounds, and feels like."
   —REV. EMILY VANDEN HEUVEL, Wedgewood Christian Services

Jolene "is a giddily frolicsome soul who enjoys getting into holy trouble."
   —from the foreword by QUENTIN SCHULTZE

Be
Mine

Be Mine

Your Invitation to God's Lavish Love

Jolene DeHeer

Foreword by Quentin J. Schultze

e

edenridge press

GRAND RAPIDS, MICHIGAN

Published by
Edenridge Press LLC
Grand Rapids, Michigan USA
www.edenridgepress.com
service@edenridgepress.com

Design by Matthew Plescher

Quantity discount pricing is available.
service@edenridgepress.com
Fax: (616) 365-5797

ISBN-10 0982706367
ISBN-13 9780982706367

Library of Congress Control Number: 2011931073

REL012030   RELIGION / Christian Life / Family

To my beloved friend Necia Vander Wall
June 18, 1952 – January 3, 2011
Who helped me understand and experience God's love

Acknowledgments

I first wish to thank Jesus Christ, the source of my joy and hope, for the privilege of serving readers. I thank him for the other sources of delight he placed in my life, such as my family and church. I thank my loving and patient husband, David, who is my greatest fan and "the wind beneath my wings." I'm grateful to our wonderful son, Jeff, and his beautiful wife, Karen, who demonstrated to me what grace looks like in person; and for our two granddaughters, Elizabeth and Katherine, who have brought more love and happiness into my life then I ever thought possible. I thank special friends who have truly been a constant source of encouragement, and my pastors, who have consistently pointed me toward Jesus.

There are three persons I would like to mention by name because without their faith and encouragement I would never have written this book. These are my soul sister and accountability partner, Necia Vander Wall, who passed away while I was working on this book and to whom I have dedicated it; my professional mentor, Quentin Schultze; and my dear friend Norm DeGraff. Each of you humbles and lifts me up. I'm deeply appreciative.

I also want to thank you for reading this book. You probably don't even know me personally and yet you have decided to spend time with me. Your graciousness makes me smile. I am always humbled and delighted when God chooses to use someone like me to help build his kingdom. I pray that this book will bless you richly.

Contents

FOREWORD

Quentin J. Schultze

The first time I met Jolene DeHeer I thought she might be daffy. My initial impression of her has now been confirmed in this book. As Jolene herself admits in the introduction, her dipstick isn't touching the oil in her crankcase. She is a giddily frolicsome soul who enjoys getting into holy trouble.

Jolene's daffiness serves her as a gifted storyteller who keenly observes the folly of everyday life in our good but goofy world. She helps us understand and appreciate our own wacky ways. Who else would tell us about the time she inadvertently asked the city water worker whether he had pants on? Who else would have taught her young son about the importance of prayer only to hear him scream "Pray for me!" as she dragged him out of the sanctuary during worship for misbehaving?

Jolene is uncannily skilled at discerning the state of modern life—from the perils of parenting to the challenge of buying lingerie from a prickly young sales clerk whose

Be Mine

bodice is smaller than the turkeys Jolene roasts for Thanksgiving. Jolene is a prophetic raconteur who tells it like it is. She thereby cautions us about straying too far from grace for fear we will cook our own gooses if not our bodices.

I learned from Jean Shepherd, who wrote the screenplay for *A Christmas Story*—about the kid who wants a Red Ryder BB gun for Christmas—there are essentially two kinds of humor. One type humbles people by fingering their hypocrisy. This kind of humor can get nasty, but sometimes it's necessary. Political cartoons often take this stand against leaders who don't walk their pompous talk. Such sardonic humor employs a sharp sword.

The other kind of humor comforts people by helping them identify with those who have gone through similar life experiences. In this style of humor, the storyteller says to the audience, "I've been there and made it back alive. You can, too. Here are a few helpful tips. Now hang on for the ride."

When you read Jolene's writings or listen to her presentations, you immediately sense she is empathetically on your side because she spoofs herself as well as others. Her self-deprecating humor is mercifully insightful. It helps us all to recognize when we are naively trying to start our engines on an empty crankcase. She admits that the only way we will get ahead in life is by humbly examining our own lives, gratefully looking to God for guidance, and faithfully moving forward. She recognizes true life as a comedy of humble faith.

The first time I heard Jolene speak, I thought she would be the next Barbara Johnson, the madcap geranium-in-the-hat lady who entertained and inspired so many people with her own stories of grace—until she passed away a number of years ago. So I filed my assessment of Jolene in the back of my mind in case I would ever have an opportunity to help her expand her ministry of speaking into a ministry of writing.

Years later, I began bugging her about writing up some of her wonderful stories. I thought they would work well in print. Jolene soon composed a fine manuscript—witty, insightful, uplifting, encouraging, and more. This book is the final result, and I am honored to have served Jolene along the way as her pest.

In this book you'll discover anew the ways God loves everyday folks in the midst of life's triumphs and tragedies. Jolene reveals her own difficult trials, including twelve miscarriages. She suffered abuse and neglect, yet refused to let her childhood dictate her adulthood—and certainly not her own parenting. She and her husband, David, were victims of business fraud, but declined to file for bankruptcy because it just didn't seem like the honorable way out of their financial predicament. As a result, they went broke. Completely broke. No-food-on-the-table broke. That was a tragedy, but it soon became a comedy (and I won't give away the story). At every turn there were people who encouraged them, and opportunities for Jolene and David to encourage others.

Jolene has discovered what all great humorists recognize, namely, their best personal stories are parables. The faithful humorist learns that life's trials are universal—and that grace is as well. Some theologians call it "common grace"

(grace for all people) and distinguish it from "saving grace." The humorist admits to us that foolishness and wisdom exist together in our lives, often side by side. Humor, as parable, helps us see that good and bad are both parts of reality—and that we often don't do a very good job of distinguishing between the two after we get up in the morning and before we retire at night. The rest of the time we do fairly well.

Shepherd used to tell me "that you can't have God without the devil." Once at Princeton Theological Seminary, Shepherd appeared on stage as the devil. It was outrageous. His point was that you can't just accept "good" without also considering "evil." But even when he performed the devil he ended up telling stories of grace; he gave the devil quite a scare that night.

In Shepherd's *A Christmas Story*, the dreamy young Ralphie manages by common grace not to shoot his eye out with the BB rifle; his eyeglasses are shattered by a ricochet, but the lenses still protect his eyes. Ralphie's mother was right, as mothers in Shepherd's stories always are—Ralphie probably shouldn't have been horsing around with the rifle. When grace shows up, potential tragedy inexplicably becomes comedy. If Ralphie had indeed shot his eye out, the movie would have ended on a tragic note—as if there were no grace for the poor kid who was just trying to shoot the neighborhood bad guys in their behinds. What's wrong with that?

Grace just happens, often against all odds and in spite of our seemingly altruistic intentions. Humor helps us to see the gap between even our best motives and the actual outcomes. Then it celebrates the fact that, given human foolishness, the outcomes were not as bad as they might have been.

For reasons I haven't quite determined, it seems that my Jewish friends often are the best tellers of comedic stories of grace. Jerry Seinfeld used to say his sitcom was about nothing. Actually, it was all about grace because the characters somehow survived the muck of confusion, pretension, and ignorance—week after week. Sometimes they even learned from their foibles. They never learned enough to become perfect friends, but certainly enough to continue to appreciate each other as varied but equally nutty individuals. What more could we expect this side of heaven?

Jolene stands with the Jewish comics as a loving observer of human folly. She deftly reveals the gap between what God expects and what we humans actually do. She also helps us laugh loudly because of her faith that things will indeed work out in the end regardless of our pitiful attempts to play god by single-handedly trying to fix everything and everyone. We love to dole out advice we ourselves don't even heed.

Yes, Jolene is daffy. I'm glad. She gives me hope for myself. If God can keep her out of excessive trouble, maybe there's a chance for me and you as well. Read this book and you'll discover what I mean. Grace is just around the corner, chapter by chapter. I'm grateful she had enough oil in her engine to crank out this delightful book.

INTRODUCTION

The setting was breathtaking. Large bay windows overlooked the sun-kissed waters of San Diego Bay. Palm trees and lush, green tropical plants framed the view. Beautiful china and stemware sparkled on the elegant white table clothes in the banquet hall at the upscale hotel. Decorative red, pink, and white hearts confirmed that we were celebrating Valentine's Day.

Over one hundred women attending the luncheon had just finished a delectable meal. Now it was time for me to deliver my (hopefully) inspiring and encouraging talk about God's love. I told my first joke and everyone laughed. It was a good beginning. The second joke elicited an even greater response. I was off and running, thanks to God's grace.

As I described God's all-encompassing love, I suggested to the women that God wants all of us to be his valentine. Everyone seemed attentive and genuinely interested, although I have learned I can't be sure if adults are actually listening to me. They're very polite, but they have the ability to look right at me and smile as they plan their weekly menu.

When my presentation was over and the women were dismissed on this Valentine's Day, a sweet, silver-haired southern belle approached me. I immediately felt a kinship with her, mostly because she was shorter than me. This rarely happens unless I'm speaking at a preschool. I was delighted for the opportunity to hear her response to my presentation and, if necessary, to clear up any confusion caused by my delivery. So I simply asked how I could help her. In her soft, southern drawl she said, "Honey, I don't know how tuh tell y'all, but I don't think yer dipstick is a'touchin' oil!"

I laughed loudly because she was absolutely correct. She pegged me perfectly. I don't think I have any oil in my crankcase or wherever you pour it in the car. I'm a tasty taco short of a combination platter. I'm a savory sandwich short of a picnic. By God's grace, I've learned not only to accept my shortcomings and my wackiness, but to celebrate them and to share them with others. This book is for everyone who's mental dipstick isn't touching oil, but who's spiritual dipstick measures how filled they are with the Holy Spirit.

So let me warn you in advance: I have an overly developed and self-deprecating sense of humor. I love to laugh, especially at myself. Put me in an embarrassing situation and I've got a story to tell the world about what's wrong with me and most likely everybody else in the zoo we call life. Sometimes I laugh just for the sake laughing—it really feels good to let my belly roll.

Moreover, I've learned that laughter can help us all gain humility, relieve stress, and celebrate life. Being able to chuckle at ourselves is effective and cheap therapy. And I don't like to part with my money. Moreover, I've heard that laughing burns calories. This is perfect for me because it's about the only exercise I enjoy.

I've also discovered that laughter is a fitting way to open up ourselves to each other and to God. Humor humbles us so we take ourselves less seriously and we can take God more seriously. This is why I thoroughly enjoy using humor to teach about God and to bring people into a closer relationship with the most humble person of all times and places, Jesus Christ. As scripture tells us, Jesus Christ humbled (or emptied) himself by coming down to earth in the form of a human being and taking on the nature of a servant (Phil. 2:8).

As I looked over the audience during my Valentine's Day message, I knew there were probably women present who didn't really know God's extravagant love. Valentine's Day can be fun for exchanging cards and being romantic, but it pales in comparison to God's self-sacrificial, unconditional love demonstrated through Jesus Christ. I could detect sadness in some women's eyes, emotional brokenness in the way they held their bodies.

We human beings all yearn to know we're beloved. We seek emotional, physical, and spiritual love. This is one of our deepest human desires. Yet I meet so many people of all ages, ethnicities, races, and socioeconomic levels who feel not only unloved but also unworthy of being loved. They can't imagine they could become anyone's beloved.

Some of these lonely people are church members. They know how to perform religious rituals and how to speak

Christian terminology, but they've never fully accepted God's love. Often they lived in families where they were routinely criticized. Sometimes they suffered from perfectionism, unable to live up to even their own standards for themselves. For whatever reasons, they've not felt much of God's love even indirectly through the kind words and gentle actions of loved ones. Deep in their hearts they are lonely individuals. Trust me, there are many such unloved souls in our congregations.

The cards and greetings we share with each other on Valentine's Day can celebrate the love between a man and a woman, among good friends, and within families. Such affection is worth celebrating. But God's love is far greater than a "Happy Valentine's Day" greeting. God's alternate valentine, the good news of the Gospel, is at the core of the Bible's message of unconditional love. God's love for his children is the purest, most self-sacrificial form of love ever expressed and received. As I show throughout this book, the Bible unmistakably describes God's ravishing love for us wayward people.

As I did for the women at the luncheon, I explore in this book God's greatest gift of love. Scripture shows that the same God who created and sustains the entire universe is the God who loves each of us dearly. This biblical valentine message can't easily be expressed in a short greeting card, but it can be written in our hearts by a gracious and humble God whose love knows no limits and who seeks us no matter where we are along life's journey.

I have no idea who you are unless you visit my website (www.jolenedeheer.com) and send me an e-mail or letter.

Introduction

I'm still trying to understand the miracle of communicating with people I may never meet. But I do know that some of you desperately need to hear God's assurance of your worth. You need to capture in your own heart the unfathomable depth of God's own love for you personally. You need to "be his" in response to God's invitation for you to "be mine."

So through this book let's together seek to understand more fully the depth and scope of God's unremitting love. I pray we will fall in love with God anew, be drawn closer to him, be assured of his perfect love, and celebrate that love with other believers in the community of beloved known as the church. You and I will experience a whole range of emotions together. We'll laugh. We'll cry. We'll celebrate. We'll experience healing. I'm very honored you chose to join me on this journey of love. From my heart to yours, thank you.

Jolene DeHeer

1

GRANNYYYYYYY!

GOD'S IMMEASURABLE LOVE

Bible camp week was over. I was on a spiritual high from seeing God work awesomely in the lives of hundreds of teenagers. But my body was worn out. I was barely able to put one foot in front of the other one. Speaking twice a day and counseling hundreds of teenagers had taken its toll. I was eager to get back home to Michigan, where I was scheduled to begin speaking that evening at a weeklong service project.

As I shuffled up to the airline ticket counter, I saw the dreaded word "canceled" by my flight listing. I approached the counter aware that the airline employee standing behind the computer had no idea how important I was and how imperative it was for me to get back to Michigan that very day. After being enlightened about my supposed importance, she kindly agreed to try to book me on a later flight on a different airline. She began madly tapping on her keyboard. She tapped and tapped. Then she tapped some more. I wondered what in the world she was up to.

Be Mine

Maybe she was cruising the Internet, answering e-mail, or playing a computer game. I waited and she tapped. Finally, she informed me she had found a seat for me on a flight leaving in ninety minutes. She quickly booked me on that flight and instructed me to proceed to the counter of the new airline to secure my boarding pass. I was relieved.

I wearily dragged my luggage to the ticket counter down the hallway, and was pleasantly surprised to discover I was only second in line. Ahead of me was a guy similarly trying to rebook his flight. The problem for me was that this bewildered traveler couldn't make up his mind about his destination. Five minutes transpired while he and the attendant chatted about different flight options. Ten more minutes went by as I listened to the two accomplish zilch. I was trying to be patient, but after another thirty minutes I was about ready to blow my fuse. When I finally managed to get up to the counter to plead my own case, the woman told me she wasn't sure she could accommodate me on the upcoming flight because it was now so close to departure time.

At that point, I lost my Christian charity. I didn't need the Fruit of the Spirit; I needed a doggone boarding pass. I firmly told her I had been second in that deplorable waiting line for forty-five minutes, all the while looking at her with desperation on my face. I explained I was not trying to sneak onto the flight at the last minute, but she and her knuckleheaded client had squandered enough time to rebook an entire flight (Well, I didn't actually say that, but I certainly felt it—and I would have thoroughly enjoyed mouthing off to her—in love, of course.). I did say I just needed to get home on time and she needed to help make it happen. She got slightly annoyed but nonetheless issued me a boarding pass. I was mostly pleasant once again, with a modicum of spiritual fruit.

But I had unwittingly made a bad mistake. I had forgotten one of the basic laws of the travel jungle: never annoy the person who dispenses boarding passes. That gatekeeper dictates your future on their cute little keyboard.

When I looked at my boarding pass I discovered it included the dreaded "S" stamp. I knew what it meant— and not "special." It designated me for being searched. I would have to stand spread eagle while some joker ran a wand around my plump body, searching for camouflaged tweezers and hidden cans of hair spray. Such searches consumed time, and I didn't have much to spare. They were also a bit embarrassing.

As I ran toward the security checkpoint I noticed something even more sinister on my boarding pass. It had not one but two Ss on it. Would I be searched twice? I was pretty certain the stamp didn't mean I was "super special." And I was right.

Not only did I receive the spread-eagle wand treatment. Officials led me behind a curtain for super-special travelers like me. This was not the entrance to the holy of holies at the airport tabernacle, although a priestly special agent did appear on the scene. I'll call her Bertha the Formidable. When she walked, the terminal floor quaked. She was a behemoth. She was an intimidating Goliath and I was a deferential David. No one could get past her if she decided not to give them space. She could wrestle a bull to the ground—not to suggest I'm quite that large. And when I saw her face I was convinced she could grow a rabbinical beard in forty-eight hours. In her deep, gravelly voice, Bertha informed me she was going to touch me uncomfortably in some private places. Then she did so. Who was I to complain? I needed to catch the departing flight immediately.

Apparently satisfied I wasn't a terrorist, Bertha cleared me to fly. I said goodbye to my new friend, dashed to the gate, and got on board seconds before attendants closed the doors. I was undeniably smelly and completely disheveled, and everyone on the plane seemed to be staring at me. I was embarrassed in so many ways that I just wanted to get to my seat quickly to lick my wounds.

Because I fly frequently, I often get upgraded to first class. I love it. I get free food, a wider seat, and enough leg room that I can put my seat back without banging into the knees of the person behind me. I also feel important in first class since I get to board early and smile at the low-class flyers as they parade down the aisle to the back of the sardine can.

But in this case my irritated friend back at the ticket counter didn't sign me up for first-class accommodations. She had assigned me to a middle seat in the last row, right next to the fetid toilets—the noisy seats behind the engines, the ones that bounce around like a roller coaster whenever the craft hits even mild turbulence. As I got to the distant row in the rear peanut gallery, the man seated on the aisle kindly stood up to let me in. He looked like Bertha's spouse. I couldn't believe it! Was this guy a sumo wrestler? Had he been planted there by security to keep watch over me?

I managed to scrunch myself into the middle seat. Then Mr. Bertha sat down, oozing his flab across the armrest that supposedly separated our seats. The only good thing about sitting in my row across from the potty was the fact that the guy seated by the window was so skinny that I could overflow into his seat without getting fresh.

Then Mr. Skinny started hacking away, coughing up phlegm and toxins that probably looked like "The Thing" under a microscope. That was enough for me. I had two options: charge up the aisle with the intent of stealing a first-class seat, or stretching my arms in front of me, closing my eyes, and praying for a strong jet stream to shorten the trip East. I desperately consigned myself to the latter option for fear that Bertha the Formidable had been seated in first class to make sure I didn't try to rush the cabin.

By God's grace, I made my connecting flight and arrived home in Grand Rapids a mere twelve hours after my journey had begun at the original ticket counter where I had been semi-kindly rebooked on another airline. I was weary, upset, and desperate to see my husband's face as I passed security and entered the public ticketing area. But he was nowhere in sight. Now I was really annoyed. "Enough is enough," I muttered to myself. Where was he? Once again, I dragged my luggage behind me, grumbling as I shuffled from the baggage claim area to the main terminal exit.

Suddenly a noise caught my attention. I looked up. Running down the concourse was the cutest little blonde-haired girl yelling, "GRANNYYYYYYY!" My granddaughter, Kate, had arrived with her grandpa to pick me up. I dropped my luggage midstream and ran to greet her. My lousy attitude melted away. I scooped up precious Kate in my arms and twirled her around. At that moment, there was no one else in the airport except Kate and me. She laid her head on my shoulder and said, "I love you so much, Granny!" This was my own "Grannyyyyyyy! experience."

Hearing Kate's excited voice, seeing her precious face, and then holding her warm body against mine were such overwhelming, immeasurable, and seemingly undeserved gifts. I was also totally overwhelmed by the depth and scope of my love for her. I felt as if my heart was too tiny to hold so much love. Right there, in the middle of the Gerald R. Ford International Airport, I suddenly realized not just how much little Kate loves me and I love her, but how much more God must love me. If Kate could be so unquestionably devoted to me, how much more loyal must God himself be toward me? My love for her was great, but God's love for me is greater still. My granddaughter's unconditional love had reminded me that God accepts me as I am, even with all my faults, like a loving father—an Abba.

I hope you have experienced God's fatherly love. We Christians often intellectually acknowledge that God loves us. But I wonder how many of us truly feel enveloped by God's immeasurable love. God sends us valentines every day, reminding us how much he loves us. My granddaughter's greeting at the airport that exhausting night was a valentine reminder to me how much God loves me.

Most of all, we hear about God's love through the Bible, God's ultimate valentine. God exclaims in scripture, "I have loved you with an everlasting love; I have drawn you with unfailing kindness" (Jer. 31:3). "The Lord your God has chosen you out of all the peoples on the face of the earth to be his people, his treasured possession" (Deut. 7:6). "I have redeemed you; I have summoned you by name; you are mine" (Isa. 43:1). "For God so loved [you!] that he gave his one and only Son, that whoever believes in him shall not perish but have eternal life" (John 3:16). What marvelous love letters.

God's special valentines ask you to open your heart to his love. God's love is so extravagant that a lifetime is too short to explore the extent of it; so he offers us eternal life to enjoy him forever. Just as God came to speak words of love through Kate to me in the airport, he wants to tell you how much he loves you personally. He seeks to assure you that you are cherished even though you (like me) act self-importantly, get impatient with others, and try to take complete control of your disorderly life. You are precious to God. Let's listen to him and celebrate his immeasurable love.

2

Are Your Pants On?

GOD'S PERSISTENT LOVE

When I became a mother, I expected the parenting to be a blessing. It was. What I didn't expect was how our son would humble me and keep me on my knees in prayer. We had only one child, Jeff, who became the joy of our lives. When he was a toddler, however, he tested the limits, pushed the envelope, and pressed our buttons.

Jeff had the ability to convert me in seconds from a relatively sane Christian adult to a screaming idiot. Jeff grabbed on to life with both hands, took control, and enjoyed nearly every minute of it. I didn't want us to squash his creative, exploratory spirit. But I didn't want myself to become a blaring banshee, either. I needed assistance. My husband and I both needed help. The task of raising Jeff was well beyond our own abilities.

Eventually I found help in the writings of James Dobson, a well-known Christian psychologist who wrote practical books on parenting. Two of his works—*The Strong-Willed*

Child and *Dare to Discipline*—became my lifelines to relative maternal sanity. I put Dobson's books right next to my Bible. Whatever he said, I believed. Only one big problem: Jeff didn't know he was supposed to act like the disciplined children in Dobson's self-help tomes. Jeff hadn't read Dobson's book! Consequently, he didn't know how Dobson said he was supposed to behave. And I wasn't about to read to Jeff at bedtime from one of Dobson's books.

Dobson confidentially says that if you give your child fifteen to twenty minutes of advance notice they'll be more than happy to change an activity to accommodate a new parental directive. What insight! "Fabulous advice," I thought to myself. "Why didn't anyone else tell me this pearl of parenting wisdom?" I accepted the advice. It sounded sensible and doable. This was a no-brainer.

So one day when I needed to go grocery shopping, I asked Jeff to change out of his soggy little swimming trunks into an adorable outfit I had placed on his bed. I informed him that in fifteen to twenty minutes we would depart for the supermarket. Being the stewardly homemaker that I sometimes was, I gathered my menu for the week, clipped some coupons, and wrote out a grocery list. I was ready to fly through the supermarket like a supermom. Little did Dobson know that his technique would give me extra time to get organized. Bonus! Jeff and I would soon be off for a pleasant trip to the grocery store, where he would impress the other moms with his darling outfit.

After about twenty minutes had elapsed, I was finished planning and was ready to call Jeff to the door so we could get in the car together. Because I am a woman of childlike faith—in God if not always Dobson—I walked confidently into my son's bedroom, fully expecting him to be prepared to depart for the store. I imagined him in his adorable outfit, jumping up and down with excitement because he got to change himself in plenty of time without his Mom hassling him repeatedly to get his act together.

Strangely, Jeff's clothes were still on the bed. In fact, he wasn't even in his bedroom. I started walking through the house yelling out the various disciplinary iterations of his name—Jeff, Jeffery, Jeffery David, and finally Jeffery David DeHeer. No response. I was not pleased. I wasn't too thrilled with Dobson, either. I wondered if Dobson really believed that *my* son, Jeffery David DeHeer, would happily change activities in fifteen to twenty minutes if I just gave him notice.

Suddenly I heard a sound outside, by the side of the house. "The little rascal is playing in the yard," I muttered to myself. I charged to the front door, threw it open, and yelled outside, "Are you running around out there without your pants on?" A deep voice answered, "No, madam. I'm here reading your water meter."

Ouch! Jeffery David DeHeer won this one. He was still scrambling around the yard in his swimming trunks and I was thoroughly embarrassed. Our children do humble us. And we parents do embarrass ourselves trying to humble our children. These are two of the laws of parenting even though I never found them in any of Dobson's books. Remember: "Parent, thy children will embarrass thee, and thee will further embarrass thyself." I don't think it would work as a title for a Christian parenting book.

Faithful parents persist through the various embarrassments and related frustrations. We don't simply give up and walk away from our children, letting them do their own thing. We stay the course. Children can break our hearts, but we don't surrender our love for them. Even when as young adults they seem to want to walk away from us and everything we hold dear, we still seek the best for them. If the twenty-minute rule is a bust, we try a different approach. We persist for years, all the way until they leave their father and their mother for their new life with someone else.

Parental persistence is something like God's persistent love for his children. God would have every right to give up on us and to punish us for a lot more than merely getting frustrated with our offspring. God would have plenty of reason to abandon his children for disobeying their father in heaven. We parents and children alike are hard-headed characters in God's drama of salvation. Why doesn't God just write us out of his script and let us fend for ourselves?

Because our God is persistently loving. His patience with us is beyond anything Dobson could claim regarding even the most perfect parents—of which I am hardly one. God is the hound of heaven. He keeps on loving and forgiving us even when we're running through the backyard naked, let alone in bathing trunks. He calls us repeatedly to get ready for eternal life. The biblical story that best helps me to understand God's persistent love is Luke's parable of the lost or prodigal son (15:11-32).

This young man in the parable had everything he could have ever wanted emotionally, socially, and physically. He was the beloved son of a wealthy man. His future was assured. All he had to do was love and obey his father. But his father's love and provisions weren't enough for him. He wanted more. For himself.

As a result of his warped desires, he acted extremely disrespectfully. He asked his father in advance for his inheritance. In Middle Eastern culture at that time, his request was like saying to his father, "Drop dead. It's my money. I want it now! My cash is more important than your love. I'd rather have you dead than wait for my rightful inheritance." Can you believe it? How could this selfish young man so thoroughly disrespect his father? How could he see his own family merely as a means to fulfill his selfish purposes? I can imagine this lost son congratulating himself as he turned his back on his family and headed down his own path. He got what he wanted—lots of money and plenty of freedom to live as he pleased.

There is something of the young son in each of us. We're similarly if not so blatantly selfish and disobedient. We deny that we belong to our father in heaven, that we're God's beloved children. We disregard the fact that our fatherly God wants to give us all we could ever need, such as peace, joy, hope, love, eternal life, and the power of the Holy Spirit.

Even if we know intellectually that we've been promised the wonderful inheritance of eternal life and that we don't need to fear the future, our deceitful hearts tell us we should desire more of whatever looks and feels good to us. We want life our way, on our terms. We want to live as if the world revolves around us instead of God. We look to meet our own needs before we consider the sufficiency of God's desires and promises.

Meanwhile, God still desires an intimate, loving relationship with us by seducing us into obedience, by smiting us with his unfathomable love. He wants us to know in our hearts, not just in our minds, that he sacrificed his only begotten son so we could live in eternal relationship with him.

Yet we still say to our heavenly father, "Drop dead, God! I'm too busy to spend my time listening to your rules and regulations. My relationships with my spouse, children, friends, church members, and colleagues are much more important to me than my relationship with you."

We don't stop there. The way each one of us lives says to God, "I have important projects to complete, a business to run, a family to care for, courses to complete, hobbies to enjoy—and besides, there is a lot more fun to be had in this world and I mean to have it. So I've got to be free of silly rules and a confusing relationship with a God that doesn't speak to me clearly and directly. Don't ask me to spend time in prayer, Bible study, and worship. The church is loaded with hypocrites, anyway."

Yet God persists in loving us in spite of our stubborn disobedience, spiritual laziness, and self-serving rationalizations. Even in the midst of our selfish living, God our father comes to us and says, "Don't worry about anything. Give me all your cares and worries. I have a plan to bless you.

But you must submit to my leading so you will choose the way of life." Even if we hear that promise and accept our responsibility for obedience, we still might not trust God. We might yet respond, "Don't get so pushy, God. I can take care of myself. I'm getting or already have a decent education, a great future, plenty of talents and skills. I'm young, good-looking, healthy, and strong. If the going gets tough, there are plenty of things I can take to help me numb the pain. I don't need you right now. I might check back with you if I ever get desperate."

Rebelliously or indifferently, we each tend to go off to a foreign land, away from our heavenly father's care. There we will eventually find ourselves alone, destitute, and forsaken—strangers in a strange land who eventually will discover that we need forgiveness. Whether we realize it now or not, God still persists in loving us. He beckons us. His arms are open wide and ready to embrace us.

As we open our hearts to God, we discover that we are truly beloved. We hear our heavenly father saying to us, "Don't worry about anything. Give me all your cares and worries." We run back to the father.

Then there's the elder son in the parable. Apparently he was a very obedient child. I resonate with that. I'm a people pleaser and a rule follower. I'm so obedient that I drive the speed limit, follow parking lot arrows, and walk through the maze of ropes at the airport check-in counter even if no one else is in line. I'm like the son who worked hard to please his father and then figured he deserved to be rewarded. I figure I deserve my godly inheritance. Bring it on!

But when the elder son sees his father's forgiving response to his disobedient brother, he's filled with bitterness and resentment. He feels slighted and unjustly treated. He can't understand why his father would be so gracious to his selfish brother, who wantonly squandered the inheritance. The older son figures he's the righteous one who's done the right thing. He's been the obedient, loving son. His disobedient brother was the one who'd broken his father's heart and wasted the family money. So why was the troublesome brother being treated better than he was? It wasn't fair!

The elder brother had a temper tantrum. Like us, he got upset because of the way the father graciously treated someone else—as if the father lacks enough grace to go around. Like some of us, the elder brother seemed to be a good and faithful person compared to his brother. We go to church on Sundays, serve on church committees, and sometimes even help the poor. We don't try to break the ten commandments. We don't sin wildly. So why would God roll out the red carpet for the untrustworthy brother who earlier rejected his father's love? Like that elder brother, we become judge and jury for God. Like the elder brother, we look highly at ourselves and lowly at other sinners. In the process, we decry God's apparent injustice toward us.

Our problem is we ignore the bigger picture of God's extravagant grace. We focus on our own needs for attention and affirmation instead of God's unending mercy toward everyone who humbly turns to him. "Never will I leave you; never will I forsake you," says the writer of Hebrews (13:5b). Nothing "will be able to separate us from the love of God that is in Jesus Christ our Lord," writes the apostle Paul to the Roman church (8:5). God makes the same promises to us as to everyone else. His grace is fair because it's available to every wayward sinner, including you and me.

So instead of looking at the two sons as wildly different, we might consider the fact that each of us acts like both of them, depending on our situation. Like the younger son, we turn our backs on the God who has already loved us and provided for us. We break God's heart by demanding the inheritance and then running off to fulfill our selfish desires. Like the older son, we get jealous about God's attention, and self-righteous about our own holiness. At times we think we are wonderfully religious people and we look down our noses at lost souls who seem to receive God's special attention unfairly.

The two brothers share a loving father. So do we. Regardless of which son we're imitating in our lives right now, our heavenly father is waiting patiently to love us back into life-giving fellowship with him and the family of God.

By God's grace—and maybe with a dash of insight from Dobson—I really couldn't stop loving Jeff even when I unintentionally embarrassed myself in front of the utility worker. I couldn't imagine giving up on Jeff simply because he hadn't read Dobson's book about getting ready in twenty minutes on his own. Thanks to God's grace, I can't imagine anything Jeff could now do as an adult that would cause me to withhold my love from him. Jeff continues to teach me so much about God's love, including how I fall short as a mother and grandmother. I'm still awed by the fact that God's love is so much greater than the deep love my husband and I feel for our own son. I'm deeply comforted and encouraged by God's persistent love. I hope that by God's grace I can continue to be (relatively) patient, kind, and forgiving if Jeffery David DeHeer himself ever imitates the darkest sides of either of the brothers in the parable.

3

When God Ran

GOD'S RESTORING LOVE

Even though our children have the capacity to humble us before God and the world, there's a time for payback. It's called adolescence. When a child goes through puberty, their parents become sources of never-ending embarrassment. To teenagers, parents seem terminally stupid, oblivious to the real world as experienced by adolescents themselves. Parents appear clueless; teens sometimes even roll their eyes at their presumably ignorant parents.

The number of activities that can cause a teenager to be acutely embarrassed is incalculable. We parents unwittingly embarrass our adolescents just by breathing in the presence of their friends. Or by being seen dropping them off at school. Or by being seen with them in a public place. Or by taking them shopping for jeans, let alone underwear and swimwear.

Thankfully we have our own little ways of paying them back for charging us with ignorance. One of the most satisfying paybacks is showing our adolescent child's friends—or better yet their boyfriend or girlfriend—our own kid's bare-bottomed, baby-on-a-towel photos. When it comes to embarrassing our offspring, this is the killer app—and we can even do it on a smart phone to demonstrate we're not rock-toting Neanderthals. Be careful with this payback strategy, however, because the child that you're mortifying is the same one who one day may be choosing your nursing home. Paybacks always run in two directions.

Fortunately, our heavenly father isn't a payback artist. Like the prodigal son's father, God welcomes his children back home without retribution or revenge. The father in the parable had plenty of reasons to give up on each son. Both beloved sons had turned against him, although in contrasting ways.

How did the father feel during the events in the parable? Insulted? Angry? Did he experience shame and guilt, blaming himself for raising such disrespectful sons? Perhaps he was just baffled by the turn of events. I even wonder why he let the younger son leave with cash in the first place. Was the father that naïve or that honorable? Maybe by giving his son the inheritance in advance the father was preparing to admonish his son. The writer of Hebrews says we should "endure hardship as discipline; God is treating you as his children. For what children are not disciplined by their father?" (Heb. 12:7). I also wonder why the father didn't send people to track down his wayward son. Whatever the father felt along the way, he eventually put his love for his sons before his own need for respectability.

If you find yourself lost in a foreign land of sin right now because of bad decisions you've made, remember that your heavenly father wants to restore your relationship with him. Regardless of how we've insulted God, God calls us to come to our senses, admit our sin, and return to the father. The key is an old-fashioned term that never goes out of style: *repentance*. Our own broken, contrite heart is one of the most fitting gifts we can offer to God. The biblical truth is we're not worthy to be called sons of God apart from God's intervention on our behalves. Jesus opens the door for us to offer our hearts promptly and sincerely to God.

The response of our heavenly father to his repentant children—to you and me—is mirrored in the actions of the father in the parable. The gospel writer Luke tells us that while the son was still "a long way off" his father saw him coming and was "filled with compassion for him" (15:20). Amazing! The father was watching and waiting. He yearned for his son to return forgiven, restored, and cherished. Similarly, our heavenly father wants to forgive us and restore us to fellowship. He desires to give us all the rights of a child of the King, including an eternal inheritance. He wants to wipe away every tear from our eyes and fill our hearts with joy and peace. God is eager to do this for us no matter how many times we've embarrassed him.

What happens next in the parable astonishes and excites me the most. The father "ran to his son, threw his arms around him and kissed him" (20). The father sprinted to his arriving son. He didn't delay and he didn't shuffle—he immediately dashed ahead. In that culture, wealthy, elderly, influential people never ran. Running was unseemly and embarrassing. If you ran at all—let alone to greet a dishonorable son—others would judge you harshly. The analogy is far from perfect, but imagine today a father or mother running out in their underwear to greet their prostitute daughter in front of the neighbors who had heard plenty of tasty gossip about the wayward daughter.

Clearly the father didn't care if others thought his actions unseemly. He didn't care if others subsequently gossiped about his unacceptable behavior. All he really cared about was the glorious fact that his son had returned home. So he dashed to his arriving son, embraced him, and kissed him. The picture takes my breath away.

I don't look pretty when I run. When I rush to greet my granddaughter at the airport, I probably resemble a pregnant rhino trying to waddle down to the watering hole. But you know what? I really don't care what I look like. I'm oblivious to what other travelers think about me. That's their problem. I have eyes only for my beloved granddaughter because I'm overwhelmed with my love for her. If she is there to greet me, I want to celebrate our love for each other by letting my emotions fly. It's my special "Grannyyyyyyyy! experience." I'm not there to please onlookers. It's time to let loose and party!

The father in the parable was overwhelmed with gratitude. His lost son was found. The child that was dead to real life was now going to flourish. That's why the father called for a celebratory feast and gave his forgiven son wonderful gifts. He offered his son the best robe, a symbol of royalty within the family. He also presented his found son with a ring, which conveyed familial authority. The father gave the prodigal son shoes for his bare feet. And the father declared it was time for the prime beef, the fattened calf, to be slaughtered in a special feast. When we return from a foreign land hurting and repenting, God welcomes us back to the community with yet one more outrageous gift—the Holy Spirit.

I love Phillips, Craig and Dean's song and a YouTube video called "When God Ran." The song takes the perspective of the returning prodigal son who recalls that "the only time I ever saw him run was when he ran to me. He took me in his arms, held my head to his chest and said, 'My son's home again.'" In the lyrics, the prodigal son adds that his father "lifted my face, wiped the tears from my eyes."

If you've ever been overwhelmed with guilt and despair, you know how heartwarming it is to be restored to close fellowship. You know how marvelous it is to have someone hold you in their arms and tell you they love you just the way you are—broken, hurting, and raw. There is no sweeter place to run than into God's own arms in prayer, letting him hold you close to his chest and tell you he still loves you and always will. When you return home to the heavenly father, restorative forgiveness will sweep over your loneliness and wash away your wounds. Don't wait. Your father is already sprinting down the path to greet you. He's not interested in paybacks, only in embarrassingly wonderful forgiveness.

4

The Ugliest Box
GOD'S HEALING LOVE

It's 9 p.m. The dishes are done, the house is picked up, the children are in bed. You're finally sitting down with a cup of your favorite tea and a good book. You offer a sigh of relief. Suddenly you hear the pitter patter of little feet coming down the stairs or hallway. Then you hear the plaintive voice of your firstborn son say, "Mom, I forgot to tell you. I told my teacher you would bring decorated cupcakes to the Valentine's Day party tomorrow. Thanks."

With his message delivered and his conscience cleared, your son returns to bed for some wonderful rest. Meanwhile, you're about to begin another half-nighter. All parents have been there. They've all managed to go the extra mile for their children without getting too angry about last-minute requests caused by a child's forgetfulness.

My generation holds many memories of school parties. It used to be that every birthday and holiday were opportunities for teachers to request parental provisions. When it came to Valentine's Day, I recall school kids distributing tiny heart candies with short messages on them; learning how to fold and cut paper into a heart shape; shuffling through a bag or envelope of valentine cards to find just the right one for a special friend. I also remember when I got a bit older how much I wanted to receive a valentine from a special person who I had eyes on at school—the one person I hoped had eyes for me, too.

On Valentine's Day in 1956, however, my heart was broken. I remember it like yesterday because it was so deeply painful. It was the day I heard and believed a horrible lie about myself. It was the day that distorted my view of myself for the next forty years. That outrageous lie so devastated my self-image that I buried the lie even as an adult until an August day many years later. The lie was this: I was not good enough to be worthy of being loved.

This pervasive lie shaped my entire personal life. I believed I was not good enough for anyone. Even years later I felt I was an inadequate wife, mother, and mother-in-law. The lie tainted how I felt about my roles in church. I considered myself an inadequate youth leader, Bible instructor, and church school teacher. The lie paralyzed me in my work as an inspirational speaker. Simply put, the message I heard about myself on that Valentine's Day convinced me I would be a lifelong failure.

I lost track of how many times, years later, I would be preparing to go on stage to speak to a group and would suddenly start thinking I couldn't continue. I would say to myself, "You're ugly and gross. No one really admires you.

Nobody truly wants to listen to you. People are repulsed by you. You embarrass God as well as yourself."

Whenever this happened, I would become spiritually and emotionally paralyzed. I couldn't even pray. I was able to open the Bible, but not to read it with an open heart and mind. I would just sit down, tears streaming down my face. The only, temporary escape from the lie occurred when someone else prayed for me. I repeatedly needed such intercession just to be able to take the stage. Without such prayer, no matter how hard I tried, I couldn't break free from the hold the lie had on me—until that August day.

I was in a dormitory room in Vancouver, British Columbia. The next day hundreds of teenagers would be arriving on campus to hear me speak at their convention. As I sat alone in my room, praying and meditating in preparation for the work God would accomplish through me, I was once again paralyzed by that damnable lie.

Soon a very close friend, Necia, came to my room to see how I was doing. She seemed to listen carefully to God. Apparently she felt that she should track me down and pray for me. In fact, she brought along another good friend, Sheri. I explained to them that I was again submitting to the lie. Necia understood what I was going through because she had prayed for me a number of times in the past when I similarly felt the horrible sense I was a worthless person who couldn't serve my audience. I told them how tired I was repeatedly fighting the same battle, and how I would love to know where that lie originated so I might confront it. They suggested we pray to God to identify the source of the lie. They assured me they would silently pray for me as I sought God's grace in prayer.

I was so eager to tackle the lie that I closed my eyes and immediately asked Jesus to show me where it came from. At first, I didn't receive any response. But then, while praying, I remembered an event I had buried for over four decades. I was nine years old when it occurred, on the day before Valentine's Day. My grade school teacher was explaining to the class we should all come to class the following day with a shoebox with a slot on the top and decorated especially for Valentine's Day. She also encouraged us to bring valentines—little cards with a simple picture and some saying such as "Be Mine"—for the people we liked.

Now, I was a profoundly lonely child and unsure how to proceed. I didn't really have any close friends at school. But there were six girls I wanted to be my friends. So on the way home from school that day I bought six valentines with my weekly allowance money.

At home, I couldn't find a shoebox or decorations. My parents were too involved in their own lives to assist me. I finally found a small square box and a piece of red crayon. I colored the box the best I could. Since I had little artistic ability, however, I knew the box looked pretty ugly.

The following morning I feigned illness to avoid going to school. My plan failed. But with every step I made towards school, I actually was getting sick. I became sicker and sicker to my stomach. I worried horribly. What if no one liked my box? What if my box wasn't good enough? I was an emotional wreck.

When I got to the classroom, I realized my artwork was even worse than I had imagined back home. We all had to place our boxes on the windowsill. My box, which seemed ugly at home, was absolutely pathetic next to everyone else's boxes. Other kids, probably somewhat with the help of their parents, had decorated their boxes with tissue paper, construction paper, doilies, ribbon, and even fake jewels. As I looked down the row of boxes, each one seemed more beautiful than the next one—except for mine. My box was like the ugly duckling. All day long, classmates mocked me about my hideous box.

Finally, the school day was almost over. I felt a bit of relief. But little did I know what would happen next. The teacher instructed each of us to put our box on our own desk. She explained she wanted us to evaluate each other's boxes. She was going to give us a list of different categories, such as "most beautiful box," "most creative use of red," and "most candy used." She even added a category for the "ugliest box." My box won that category.

As if that weren't upsetting enough for me, the teacher then instructed us to put our valentine cards in the slot on top of each other's boxes. After I quickly put my cards in the boxes of the six girls I wanted to befriend, I ran to the girl's bathroom. I couldn't bear to sit at my desk. What if no one placed a valentine in my box? Soon the dismissal bell rang, but I stayed in the bathroom longer. I waited there until I was confident everyone was gone from the classroom. Then I returned to my empty room and retrieved my ugly red box.

Be Mine

I didn't have the courage to open the box. I tucked it under my arm and shuffled home, worrying the whole time. I immediately went to my bedroom and shut the door. To this day, I can still see the pattern the wintry frost painted on the window. I can recall the blue wall and the feel of the chenille bedspread. Most of all, I can still experience the pit in my stomach and the fear in my heart that engulfed me back then as I pondered the contents of my horrible box.

Eventually I gained enough courage to lift the lid of the box. Sure enough, it was empty. I had no valentines. Not even one. I wasn't good enough. No one liked me. No one really wanted to be my friend. At that very moment I accepted the devilish lie that I was unworthy of being loved. I believed that lie like Eve believed the serpent. I let that lie settle into my heart and shape my self-image for decades.

After that, I definitively believed I was worthless at everything I did. I saw myself as a born loser. I hurt so intensely, however, that just to cope with my feelings I concluded I had to bury the memory. I didn't dare bring it up with anyone, even my parents. How could I? They might agree with the lie! After all, my teacher apparently did.

All of these events and experiences flowed into my memory years later as I prayed to God for insight into the source of the lie. In the Vancouver dorm room, Necia and Sherri listened to my recollections and then encouraged me to return to prayer. They suggested I offer the bad memory to Jesus so I might receive his healing. I concurred even though I wasn't sure it would make any difference.

So in my mind's eye, I was nine years old again, carrying the ugly little valentine box. But this time I wasn't trekking to school; I was walking up to Jesus, who was standing in front of a cross. When I came close to him, he reached his hand out for the box. Initially, I held back, but his compassionate eyes melted my heart and I handed him the box. Just as I placed it in his hands, the most amazing thing occurred. He touched the box and it became encrusted with rubies, diamonds, gold, and pearls. It was truly the most beautiful box I'd ever seen.

Was all of this a prayer? A daydream? A prayerful daydream? I don't know exactly. But it continued.

Jesus handed the box back to me and said, "Open it." At first I resisted, but once again his eyes warmly compelled me. I slowly lifted the lid.

I can't adequately describe what happened next because my mind and heart were swamped with emotions. All I can say is I suddenly felt infused with a powerful, overwhelming sense of being loved. I immediately became aware that I was personally worthy of being loved. As I sat there in prayer, I felt waves of love gently washing my soul, dissolving my painful memories. I experienced God's love like a healing balm on my wounded soul. It seemed like everything I had read in scripture about God's love was overwhelmingly true and real to me.

I hope that you're not living a lie about yourself. Yet I know that all of us experience the devil's deception. If you're living with a self-destructive lie that is harming your life, I encourage you to seek God's healing love with a pastor or faithful friends. Surround yourself with people who truly love you as you are. You might not experience the kind of healing I did. But by reading the Bible and participating in worship with faithful brothers and sisters in Christ, God will reveal to you over time more and more about Jesus' love and your intrinsic value as a child of God. As you discover the sources of your own self-destructive tendencies, talk with Jesus and Christian friends about them. If necessary, seek professional counseling. Otherwise the negative effects of lies in your life might continue for decades, as they did for me.

One type of Bible-based prayer that has helped me commune openly with Jesus is the spiritual discipline of *Lectio Divina*. It's a way to listen to God and pray scripture. This type of prayer, which focuses on scripture, might help you identify and eliminate the lies in your own life.

You may never have had your heart broken like I did on that Valentine's Day decades ago. But like all of us, surely you wish to be deeply, unconditionally loved. I hope you find such love among family and friends. But if you want the deepest love of all—truly eternal and totally uncon-ditional love with no strings attached and no chance for human disappointment—the most important person to turn to in love is Jesus Christ. God wants to tell you every day, not just on Valentine's Day, how much he loves you. I continue to need God's healing love to restore my spirit and fill me with joy. I still become fearful and anxious. Old habits and haunting memories die hard. But now I am eager each night to open my Bible and hear God's voice tell me how precious, treasured, and beloved I really am. God's unconditional love is the most beautiful of all.

5

Did You Flush?
GOD'S SACRIFICIAL LOVE

Mothers understand the meaning of sacrifice. Their parental sacrifices begin even before their first child is born. And the sacrifices continue. Mothers give up a flat, unblemished stomach for an abdomen resembling a topographical map of the moon's surface. They relinquish uncountable hours of sleep. They trade looking well in stylish outfits for clothing that won't look any worse when it's layered with stains produced by liquids from either end of a baby's body. Mothers replace signature perfumes with baby lotion. They sacrifice stimulating adult conversations for phrases such as "Did you flush?" and "Please don't eat your boogers."

And those are only the beginning of maternal sacrifice. Before they know it, mothers don't have time to read what they enjoy because they have to reread Dr. Seuss for the umpteenth time. For a while, many moms give up going to the bathroom by themselves. They can hardly remember soaking in a luxurious bubble bath and shaving their legs in private. A romantic evening with their spouse is a mere concept. They hear the same kids' TV jingles over and over again.

Mothers intimately know sacrifice. For the most part, they've loved the sacrificial journey. Especially in retrospect, it provides many hours of entertaining stories.

One of the toughest maternal sacrifices, however, is learning to let go of a child. For nine months a mother carries, nurtures, breathes, and eats for a pre-born baby. She feels the first movements inside of her. She experiences the kicks—especially when trying to get to sleep. Then the doctor cuts the umbilical cord. Separation begins. Pretty soon the mother has to leave her precious bundle with a grandparent for a few hours. The separation continues. Eventually the child starts crawling away as well as toward its mother. Then walking. Then running to and fro.

Before long is the first day of school. Usually the mother, more than the father, watches the child heading to school and feels a pit in her stomach and warm tears running down her cheeks. She waves proudly but also sadly to her baby, who might not even look back to see how mom is doing. At this point, mother is no longer the center of the child's universe because teachers and friends have entered the child's life in more intense and time-consuming ways.

When adolescence finally comes, a beloved child starts preferring to be around almost anyone other than embarrassing parents. Sleepovers further supplant personal motherly attention. The same mixed emotions recur if the child heads to college or marries.

My adult son's dating and eventual wedding called for a lot of sacrifices, both wonderful and challenging. I got to experience the joy of having our son bring home a beautiful young woman whose waist was thinner than my thigh. She hadn't gone through the difficult hours of labor that I did just to deliver my son to her eventual embrace. She didn't experience the joy of being anointed while changing his diapers. She didn't have to experience calluses on her knees from praying and agonizing over every bump in her boyfriend's journey from childhood through adolescence.

It all seems to work out in the end, however, because I gained a wonderful daughter-in-law without having to potty train her or cover the tab for her braces. I got to experience God's faithfulness in providing a splendid wife for my own son. I witnessed my son's adult pleasure in falling in love with the person who would become his wife. Finally, along with my many sacrifices for my son, I was eventually able to experience the most amazing gift of grandchildren.

In spite of all of the benefits to sacrificing for children, none of it begins to compare to the benefits for us all of God's sacrificial love. I can't fully wrap my mind around it, but God let his only son die for us because he loves us so much (John 3:16). As a parent, I get inklings of this kind of self-sacrifice; I did sacrifice for my son because I love him so much. But beyond that analogy is the unfathomable nature of God's fatherly sacrificing for us. For one thing, I can't conceive of any parent, let alone God, sacrificing their own child. The thought itself grips my heart. For another thing, I can't even imagine any parent just thinking about taking the life of their own beloved child. How in God's name could the very Creator of the universe plan for the death of his only son? How could he carry it out? Why was it even necessary?

My husband and I have only one child. Along the way, however, we lost twelve children through miscarriages. Twelve different, individual children. Our son, Jeff, is our miraculous gift from God. I feel like the love we had for all of our children who never made it into the world became directed at Jeff. My husband and I deeply love one another, but we didn't conceive each other. We conceived Jeff. We "begat" him, not in the way the creator begat his only son, but perhaps with similar gratitude.

In a special, motherly way, I gave Jeff life. This is why I can't even imagine letting Jeff die so someone else could live. Jeff is my one and only child. So given all I've been through in the many miscarriages and eventually the miraculous blessing of Jeff, I am completely astonished at the very idea that God himself, the creator and sustainer of the universe, would love us so much that he would give his only son for the sake of us, a deeply rebellious people. From a purely human perspective, this kind of love makes no sense to me. Our Jeff is a miracle, but the death and resurrection of Jesus Christ are beyond even miraculous understanding. Jesus Christ represents a kind of love that doesn't quite compute. It can't be analyzed as much as accepted and enjoyed.

I've tried to imagine what it must have been like for God to observe how humanity rejected his beloved son. How did God feel when people lied about, mocked, rejected, and abandoned Jesus? How could God even bear to watch wicked men spitting upon the Lord, beating him with a staff, slapping his raw face, scourging his back, pressing thorns into his scalp, and then nailing his precious hands and feet to a cross as if he were a criminal? How could God accept such savage treatment let alone foresee it?

Even more amazing to me is the fact that God had the power to stop Jesus' agony. As a parent, I did all I could to keep Jeff from being physically or emotionally traumatized. As he grew up, there were many times when he was not with us and we didn't have the immediate power to protect him if such unfortunate situations would have arisen. But God was present when his only son was tortured and killed. Why didn't he intervene?

God stood on the sidelines, not because he didn't love his son enough, but because he loves us so much. God knew how to deal with the disobedience of generation upon generation of human beings. He would give us a life-giving relationship with him by destroying our sin through the death of his own, innocent son. Jesus took our sins upon himself. The necessary sacrifice on our behalf had to be truly holy, yet truly human. The only one to fit that bill was God's one and only son, Jesus Christ. God let go of his son in order to surrender him for us. Jesus thereby became our sacrificial lamb.

In turn, Jesus demonstrates his sacrificial love on the cross by obeying his father. Jesus Christ was fully human, so he must have experienced the sins of the world in the agony of the cross. I appreciate Aaron Shust's song, "My Savior, My God," that says, "He who lives to be my King once died to be my savior." When I sing that line, my mind recalls images from the film *The Passion of the Christ*. Of course the movie is a Hollywood version of what actually occurred on Calvary. But it helps drive me to my knees with gratitude and humility. Jesus obediently stayed the course under the faithful watch of his father in heaven. Jesus' love for the father and for us kept him on the agonizing path to the cross. Jesus thereby became the greatest of friends for you and for me. Jesus told his own disciples that "greater love has no one than this: to lay down one's life for one's friends" (John 15:13).

God's own sacrificial love in Jesus Christ is the overwhelming evidence that we are worthy of being loved. There is no way God would have sacrificed his only begotten son if we were not worthy of Jesus' atoning love. Christ's sacrifice was—and is—our redemption. Christ's sacrifice reveals how precious, beloved, and highly valued we are to God himself.

Left to our own devices, we aren't so inclined or equipped to love others. Sure, most mothers do tend to their children. Yes, most fathers do serve their sons and daughters. Perhaps of all institutions, families most demonstrate sacrificial love. But isn't it true that we all have a lot of trouble sacrificing ourselves for others? Don't we wonder if it's worth it? Don't we give up on some people—even entire groups of people we stereotypically put in the "no hope" category? How well do we reach out to the most needy in our communities—the abused, the lonely, the unemployed, the destitute, the widowed, the terminally ill, and the prisoner?

Even if we know intellectually that every person is made in God's image and worthy of our love, we lack the will to become truly self-sacrificial followers of Jesus Christ. It's just not in our nature. So God gives us the Holy Spirit to soften our hearts and form our wills in tune with God's own sacrificial love. The Spirit shows us the way to put others' needs ahead of our own, to deny ourselves, and to count everything rubbish compared with being obedient to Jesus Christ. By submitting to the power of the Holy Spirit, we become godly lovers. Only the Spirit's power can equip us to love others as we love ourselves.

According to one popular story on the Internet, a hospital volunteer got to know a little girl named Liz, who was suffering from a rare and serious disease. Her only chance of recovery appeared to be a blood transfusion from her young brother, who had miraculously survived the same disease and had developed the antibodies needed to combat the illness.

The doctor explained the situation to her brother, and then asked the boy if he would be willing to give his blood to his sister. The volunteer saw the brother hesitate for only a moment before taking a deep breath and saying, "Yes, I'll do it if it will save her."

As the transfusion progressed, the boy lay in bed next to his sister and smiled as the color returned to her cheeks. Then his face grew pale and his smile faded. He looked up at the doctor and asked with a trembling voice, "Will I start to die right away?"

Of course not! But this young boy nevertheless saw that the deepest of all love is sacrificial. It's the kind of love whereby we give away our time, energy, and sometimes even our blood. This is the kind of love we Christians should desire and practice. The Holy Spirit calls us to accept God's abundant love so we can be a love-filled blessing to others.

Mothers and fathers sacrifice for their children. But even such maternal and paternal love can't begin to compare to the sacrificial love God offers us. If you become complacent about the scope of God's love, if you don't feel the Spirit stirring in your heart, remember God's own self-sacrifice. If you doubt that God loves you or you are worthy of his love, remember the cross. In the depth and scope of God's sacrifice you discover that you are beloved, and you'll be inspired by the Holy Spirit to love others as Jesus loves you.

6

Oh, Precious Lord

GOD'S EMPOWERING LOVE

We've all experienced situations that seemed totally beyond our ability to handle. I remember the first time I spoke to an audience of three thousand teenagers. The ministry that hired me had never asked a woman to speak at its conferences, partly because the staff was not sure a·woman could handle an audience of thousands of sugar-hyped, hormone-charged, sleep-deprived teenagers going bonkers. I was honored by their invitation and fairly confident I could hold the attention of that many potentially unruly adolescents.

Unlike adults, teenagers let you know right up front if they aren't listening; they just start texting on their phones, looking out the window, yawning, fidgeting, talking, or noticeably snoozing. Teens don't even care if you see them ignoring you. I really enjoy speaking to teens because they can be so honest. I can read them while speaking and then adjust my delivery as needed to keep them attentive.

After arriving at the venue, I went to the empty auditorium to perform sound checks. As I looked at the vacant auditorium, I imagined thousands of teenagers doing the wave—a fun and engaging group activity in which different audience sections consecutively raise their hands in the air, creating a wave-like flow across the audience. I thought to myself, "How would I stop that many people from doing an activity like the wave?" I really didn't know. And what began scaring me was the fact that I had seen audiences getting so involved in the wave that speakers couldn't get the audience under control; the wave took over. My confidence in myself as a speaker started evaporating. Fear began capturing my mind.

I thought to myself, "Who do I think I am? What am I trying to do? I can't control that many teenagers!" I started hyperventilating. My heart was palpitating. Panicked, I did the only thing I knew could help me. I dashed to my room, prayed, and read the Bible.

I realized that I could get through this kind of large event only by the grace of God and the power of the Holy Spirit. So I poured out my heart to God, asking him either to remove me from the situation or to give me grace to proceed with the events. I read 2 Corinthians 9:8, "And God is able to bless you abundantly, so that in all things at all times, having all that you need, you will abound in every good work." What a promise! I believed that those words were meant for me personally. So I simply prayed to God for the ability to keep the kids from uncontrollably doing the wave.

On the first day of the five-day event, I hesitantly walked on stage. But by God's grace, I quickly connected with the warmly responsive audience. There was no wave. On the second day, still no wave. Hallelujah! On the third and fourth days, I was on a roll. No wave. I could tell I was regaining my confidence. Maybe I was even becoming overconfident. I knew down deep I was paying less attention to the real source of my effectiveness—the Holy Spirit—and more attention to my own rhetorical skills.

As I walked up on the stage for the last meeting, teenagers were already shouting in unison, "We love you, Jolene!" I was so thrilled. I tried to be as humble as possible while they chanted, but evidently someone in the audience determined that I needed to be taken down a couple notches. Maybe a trickster in the back row said to himself, "Dude, if we can, like, yell together, I bet we can all do the wave." So he started leading the people seated around him in the wave; within seconds, everybody in the audience was doing it.

There it was, right in front of me. A wave. Then another wave. My worst fears were coming true. Try to imagine yourself standing alone on a huge stage with thousands of teenagers and their leaders looking at you while they're furiously creating wave upon wave from one end of the auditorium to the other.

I began praying silently to God as the waves undulated in front of my petrified body. I told God I was clueless about how to respond to the adulatory waves. I prayed something like this, "Dear God, do you remember 2 Corinthians

9:8—about your blessings and my good works? Of course you do, since you inspired those words. You promised blessings at all times. Well, now would be a good time."

I lifted my head and peeked out. They were still rolling out waves. I silently continued, "Lord, look out there. Do you see what I see? Yes, it's the wave. And I'm clueless how to stop it." I peeked again. The pack of three thousand youth was still doing it. My prayers intensified, rivaling those of old-time evangelists. "Oh, precious Lord. If ever I needed you, I need you now. Show me what to do. Please!"

I ceased praying, looked up, and slowly raised my right hand as if I were stopping traffic. I didn't say a word. I didn't mouth a word. I just stood there, arm raised, hand up in the air. And they stopped! I couldn't believe it. What happened? God did it. I felt power like I've never felt it before. I had just done the impossible with God's help. I felt like Moses parting the waters. All it took was a raised hand, yet I was oblivious until the Spirit intervened. The Lord had taught me. I thought to myself that I should remember this commanding action.

Several weeks later, my husband and I were heatedly discussing something that I've long since forgotten. I remembered what to do. Employing my newfound power, I raised my hand just as my husband started adamantly defending his position. He just looked up at me like I was goofy. Then he asked if I'd recently joined a fascist group. Whoops! Wrong move. An angry spouse isn't the same as a jubilant teenage crowd. I still lacked an awful lot of discernment when it came to using hand signals wisely.

I learned as a clueless speaker in front of thousands of electrified teens I still needed supernatural power to overcome seemingly impossible situations. There was no way I could prepare for every contingency when I walked out on stage. I was at the Lord's mercy in spite of how well I had served audiences previously. My own stirring elocution was hardly sufficient. I desperately needed the Holy Spirit to guide me.

We all face times when we're asked to do the impossible—to endure a divorce, to say goodbye to a loved one, to contend with terminal illness, to work through a job loss, to watch a child walk away from God, to deal with injustice or prejudice, to overcome anxiety and depression, or even to handle traumatizing childhood experiences. When such calamities strike, we want to run away, cover our heads, and avoid coming up for air. We feel alone, vulnerable, and fragile. We don't have the energy or desire to try to tackle the situation. For many people, including me, the speaker extraordinaire, public speaking can be petrifying.

In such situations we need to remember and believe that we don't have to rely solely on our own, puny efforts. We have the promise of 2 Corinthians 9:8: "God is able" to do what we can't accomplish ourselves. God is able to save us, to sanctify us, and to send us into formidable situations to serve him successfully by the power of the Holy Spirit. God delights in pouring out his grace upon us in the service of others.

God doesn't just give us a tiny bit of grace. He lavishes grace—abounding grace, enabling grace, grace that empowers us to do scary but good works such as being faithful in the midst of our messy lives. He gives us grace so that in all things and at all times we will have all we need to abound in every good work. Now that's empowering love!

If you're going through a seemingly impossible situation, let the knowledge of God's empowering love fill your heart with hope, comfort, and encouragement. Allow his love to strengthen your faith. Rely on his love to help you face these tasks, knowing you are enveloped in his grace and filled with his power. Whatever you need to accomplish, you don't have to do it alone. God doesn't even want you to go it alone.

Your life might be going smoothly now, but when you face a devastating circumstance don't give in to the tendency to hide. Remember the promise of 2 Corinthians 9:8. Remember that God delights in empowering you to do the impossible. Face difficulties with assurances that you are empowered by God. Trusting in him and relying on his love will lead you through trials. As you later look back on those difficult times you'll probably proclaim that "with God all things are possible" (Matt. 19:26).

Facing our trials, including our hurts, isn't easy. But one of the great messages of the Bible is that God's grace is more than sufficient for us. When we obediently trust him, we discover that the reward of being obedient is much greater than the effort expended to be obedient. The outcome of our efforts isn't determined by our weakness, but by God's grace.

God has the power to transform our most miserable situation into a blessing. According to what might be an urban legend but is nevertheless an inspiring story, a mother at a concert being performed by the great Polish pianist Ignacy Jan Paderewski realized that her child was missing just as the curtains parted and the spotlights focused on the impressive grand piano on the stage. The panicked mother saw her own son sitting at the keyboard, picking out, "Twinkle, Twinkle, Little Star."

Then Paderewski walked over to the keyboard and whispered in the boy's ear, "Don't quit. Keep playing." Paderewski reached down with his left hand and began filling in a bass part as the boy continued plunking single keys. The two of them together transformed what could have been an embarrassing situation into a wonderfully creative experience.

Those of us who follow Jesus Christ are never on our own. God is always with us, creating good works beyond what we can imagine. The apostle Paul wrote to the church at Ephesus that "we are God's workmanship created in Christ Jesus to do good works that God prepared in advance for us to do" (2:10).

When you face seemingly insurmountable odds, don't rely just on your own abilities. Depend on God's empowering love to direct you. Whether you're facing three thousand teenagers doing the wave or a catastrophic event in your life, God will provide. His arms are always around you and his voice is encouraging you not to quit, but to keep performing with him.

7

Pray For Me!
GOD'S FORGIVING LOVE

God gives us children partly to teach us forgiveness. Toddlers and teenagers are particularly good teachers on this topic. They can transform a sane, loving Christian adult into a screaming banshee in less than sixty seconds. Kids' behaviors can elicit unacceptable parental reactions requiring forgiveness.

I discovered that children learn early that most parents won't physically discipline their beloved offspring in front of friends at church. Before the advent of children's worship, parents and toddlers had to sit together in harmony for the entire worship service. This wasn't a problem if one's child was obedient. But what a predicament it was for those of us whose children easily grew bored and couldn't sit still!

If you've ever experienced taking children out of church because of their poor behavior, you'll empathize with me. Every parent realizes the importance of disciplining an unruly child. But single people and married couples without children might not recognize how important it is for parents to make sure their kids "look good" and "behave well" in church. One trick of the parenting trade is taking a child out of the worship service when he or she first starts misbehaving. I've done it many times. I simply clutched my child close to my chest, smiled sweetly to the congregation, and pretended that my son and I were leaving the service to visit the bathroom. Eventually I figured out that every parent had the same ruse so that we all knew what was really going on.

I'll never forget the day our son, Jeff, gave me a splendid opportunity to practice forgiveness. Jeff was never a complacent child. To him, life was far too interesting to sit still. So when he was too disruptive in church I would walk with him down the aisle with a smile on my face so I could deliver a private, three-point message to him in the narthex about how important it was to sit quietly in church so people could worship Jesus rather than focus on Jeffery. A quick message usually solved the problem for that service. We would quietly return to the sanctuary and all would be well until the pastor's benediction, when Jeff was ready to shoot like a bullet to the juice and cookies.

Occasionally he would continue to misbehave after we had had our little visit in the narthex. Then I would have to walk him out a second time, pretending that the initial bathroom run might not have done the job. During our second huddle, I usually applied a little affirmative action to his posterior. That physical sacrament was all it took and he would nicely attend to his manners the rest of the service. One Sunday morning, however, Jeff just couldn't sit still. We had completed our two visits to the "bathroom."

This particular Sunday we would have to walk rather obviously down the aisle for a record third huddle in one service.

I was ticked off. Really ticked off. Not just at Jeff—but also about my own embarrassment at having to make the faux bathroom hat trick run when the entire congregation knew what was going on. I firmly grasped his collar to make it clear I meant business even though I continued smiling to the watchful parishioners as if Jeff merely had a triune bladder problem. Little did they know what I was actually praying to myself, "Dear Lord, don't let me harm this miscreant on church property."

That third walk with him from the front of the church to the narthex seemed like an eternity. Clearly Jeff didn't want to be taken out again, probably because he feared the consequences even though this was new disciplinary terrain for both of us. Just as we approached the rear of the sanctuary, Jeff apparently experienced an epiphany based on an earlier conversation the two of us had had that week regarding prayer. He yelled out for the whole congregation to hear, "Pray for me!" Everybody burst into laughter. The minister even stopped preaching, leaned over the pulpit, and laughed so hard the pulpit shook. I was deeply embarrassed and incredibly angry. At that point, Jeff indeed needed every prayer he could get.

Did I forgive Jeff? Of course. Today I can even chuckle about the whole incident—and use it as effective public speaking material. I forgave him quickly because I love him. There is nothing he could do that I wouldn't forgive. After all, he's my son, my only child, and my love for him is boundless. Only another parent can understand such love.

Be Mine

Maybe the kind of love a parent has for a child is as close as we can come to understanding the way God loves us. It's the type of love that seeks to remove the barriers keeping two parties apart—barriers caused by jealousy, offensive remarks, disrespectful attitudes, disobedience, pride, and every other relational sin. That's what forgiveness does. It removes separation; it brings the parties back together because they want to live in communion with one another. They hate estrangement and separation.

Sadly, many of us are living with barriers we've erected or others built for us. Such barriers simultaneously divide us from each other and from God. Some of us have been so deeply hurt that we're desperate not to feel similar pain again. We try to protect ourselves by building a wall to hide behind. Separation seems like the only way we can survive the crushing heartache and humiliation of broken relationships. Somehow we think we'll be safer behind a barrier. We convince ourselves that if we stay hidden we won't have to face the cause of our grief or hurt. Eventually we discover that though it's a little bit safer behind a wall it's also profoundly lonely. Barriers bury us in loneliness. I know. I lived behind a self-constructed brick wall for the first nineteen years of my life.

I remember laying the first brick. When I was about three years old my parents were arguing vehemently about something I had done, and I felt responsible for their antagonism. As my father slammed the door to go to work, my mother banged a bottle on the counter in frustration, seriously lacerating her hand. I watched in terror the blood pouring out of her wound. I ran after my father, yelling,

"I hurt my mommy! I hurt my mommy!" I was filled with guilt, fear, and shame. Since I never wanted to experience that kind of terror again, I started erecting my wall.

As years passed, people would say things to me that made me want to hide. Their cruel taunts and teasing caused me to add brick after brick to my wall, which became a fairly effective barrier to keep others from getting close to me and potentially hurting me. As long as I didn't get too emotionally close to other people, I figured, I wouldn't get caught making a mistake or embarrassing others or myself. I wouldn't have to face anger and disappointment. If I avoided relationships, I wouldn't have to worry about my own relationships causing pain for me or others. I would rather be lonely than hurt.

During my adult years, it became increasingly clear to me I had adopted a bogus strategy for avoiding pain. The fact was I was already hurting while I was hiding behind my wall. I had thought the barrier was keeping pain out, when in fact it was actually keeping the pain inside me. I was dwelling in emotional agony, self-doubt, and self-loathing. Profound loneliness was my constant companion. And I never had the courage to speak up when others made fun of me or took advantage of me. I just retreated behind the same old wall. During that time I undoubtedly did things that broke God's heart. I simply wasn't caring for myself let alone for others. What good was that kind of wall?

As I look back on those years, I realize that I didn't really understand God as a loving father. My notion of God was far too legalistic and impersonal. I couldn't imagine Jesus' sacrifice on the cross as final payment for my sins. I didn't realize that God's love applied to a miserable, unwanted, broken sinner like me. I knew I was a problem, but I didn't see God as the solution, only as a judge.

God miraculously reached across my wall to the core of my desolate life. He tore down that wall so I could experience his ravishing love and thereby deepen my love for other people. God's forgiveness shattered my brick wall. His love of me, a sinner, allowed me to experience the kind of intimacy with others I had longed for all my life. Every one of us longs to love and be loved. Thanks to solid preaching, worship, Bible study, fellowship, and honest personal prayer, I increasingly experienced God's love and opened myself to others' love. Today I celebrate the freedom to love God in return by living boldly and confidently for him. I build bridges rather than walls.

I wonder if you're living with barriers you constructed or others built for you. I wonder if you're building walls because of fear: fear of failing; fear of not being good enough; fear of being rejected; fear of being hurt. I wonder if you're laying down bricks of guilt: guilt over a past indiscretion; guilt for hurting someone; guilt for not measuring up to expectations placed on you by others or yourself. Finally, I wonder if you're constructing your wall higher with bricks of doubt: doubt that anyone could ever love you; doubt that God is real; doubt that God could ever truly love you; doubt that God's power is strong enough to forgive you.

Or perhaps you've never realized how easy it is to erect barriers between yourself and God. Just ponder for a moment those aspects of your life that you think you can conduct secretly, beyond God's watchful eyes and ears. What do you honestly think you can hide from God? Maybe your own barriers aren't very high because your life has been relatively free of heart-wounding experiences that could have drawn you into yourself. Perhaps one of your walls has been in place so long you've completely forgotten about it. Are there any people you absolutely refuse to communicate with? Why? Who's the problem? Is there some personal sin you've had for years and have been too frightened to identify before the face of God?

Even as I was dragging Jeff out of church he knew I loved him (at least he prayed I did). After disciplining him the third time that Sunday, I also offered him my forgiveness. I was too hard on him. Did he forgive me? He did. Children can be remarkably forgiving and trusting. When someone offers them a gift, they willingly accept it. We adults, on the other hand, too often lose the ability to freely and graciously accept gifts—even gifts like love and encouragement. Yet God lovingly pursues us and freely gives us the gift of the cross of Jesus Christ, the source of all forgiveness.

If the walls between you and God are formidable, take the first step toward dismantling them by accepting God's forgiveness. Acknowledge that you caused God embarrassment, but also accept forgiveness. Not the idea of forgiveness. Not doctrine. But heart-to-heart forgiveness. Verbalize your gratitude by thanking God through Christ for his pardon. Don't just think it, but also say it from your heart. The next time you're in church, if there is a time of confession during the service, offer your sins from your heart.

For most of us who are accomplished wall builders, accepting God's forgiveness is only the start. We also have to forgive ourselves. Here's where the gift of the Holy Spirit is so important. It's really difficult to forgive ourselves without the prompting of the Holy Spirit. Ask the Spirit to empower you to set aside anything blocking your relationship with God, including your belittling attitude toward yourself. The more fully you experience God's gift of forgiveness, the more gratefully you'll love God, others, and yourself.

If you just can't seem to accept God's forgiveness and to forgive yourself, you'll benefit from help beyond the immediate intervention of the Holy Spirit. Look at it this way: sometimes the Holy Spirit works by directing us to those who can best help us. Occasionally we just have a very difficult time identifying the barriers and addressing broken relationships. Seek out the help of a pastor or counselor. Ask around for recommendations from other people; you'll be surprised at how many seemingly "normal" friends and acquaintances have benefited from counseling (you'll have plenty of great company). The best of all counseling will address both your "vertical" relationship with God and your "horizontal" relationships with other people and yourself.

Just remember along the way that God wants what you want by the power of the Holy Spirit, namely, life-giving forgiveness. As Psalm 51 puts it, God so forgives us that he makes us "whiter than snow" (7). Or as Psalm 103 declares, God removes our sins as far as the east is from the west and remembers them no more (12, 16). It's as if God wrote our sins on magicians' flash paper, touched a flame to the paper, and caused all of the sins written on the paper to completely disappear. When you accept God's forgiving love, your sins totally vanish from God's eyes.

Whether you've acted like a toddler in church who needed to be taken out and disciplined, or you're living a life filled with shame, loneliness, doubt, and fear, God will forgive you. To begin dismantling your brick wall, start with that old-fashioned practice of repenting. Let God know straightaway you're truly sorry and you're grateful for his promise of unconditional forgiveness. Be sincere, as if the wall doesn't exist. Soon it won't. God's forgiving love is that sweet.

8

Up, Up, and Away
GOD'S TRANSFORMING LOVE

I remember the old Superman comic books and television show from the 1950s. It was so satisfying for me to see good conquering evil in every story. I was especially captivated by the way Clark Kent, a mild-mannered reporter, would be transformed into Superman. My childhood friends and I would pin towels around our necks and run through the house repeating the phrase that Superman chanted every time he took off flying: "Up, up and away!" Some of us would jump off beds and sofas attempting to fly. According to news reports, some kids even leaped off small buildings, only to discover that no matter how earnestly they repeated the magical phrase they couldn't become superheroes. Those were expensive lessons.

As we grow older, we look beyond fairytales and cartoons for other ways to be magically transformed. When I was in high school, one of the female fashion fads was to wear wigs (full hairpieces) or wiglets (partial hairpieces designed to add to your existing natural hair). These fake hairpieces transformed even the thinnest, most lifeless hair into a work of art. They also magically eliminated graying hair. It seemed like everyone, regardless of their natural hair, sported hairpieces. Kids who happened to get up in the middle of the night to go to the bathroom would get spooked by their mother's hair sitting on the edge of the sink; in the dark, wigs resembled large crawly critters. Women stored extra wigs in their bedroom closets and drawers—wigs seemed to be stashed everywhere.

Ten years later, nearly all wigs disappeared, even from garage sales. Rumor had it they worked better than kindling for starting fireplace and campground fires. Some Christians were behind the times; one female televangelist continued wearing wigs throughout the 1980s and '90s. Her wigs arose into the heavens like the Tower of Babel. Somehow she must have thought she was in fashion.

I bought my first full hairpiece when I was sixteen, after I was finally asked out on a date. Back then, girls never asked guys out. As a datable girl, you had to wait until some guy figured out how cool you were and asked you for a date. It took the unobservant guys in my hometown quite a while to realize what a fine catch I would be, but some young genius finally experienced a romantic epiphany and asked me to go dancing. I was unbelievably excited. I earnestly sought to impress him. I knew this could be the start of something big and wonderful.

Because my hair is thin, I've always kept it short. During the age of wigs, I secretly longed to be able to turn my head to the side and flip my long hair over my shoulder. For some reason—perhaps because I saw it on TV or movies—I actually believed that guys found this female flip particularly exciting, even a bit stimulating, if you know what I mean. So I decided to get a full, long, blonde wig. No mere wiglet for me. I got the whole enchilada. My new wig had the power to turn any woman into a blonde bombshell. The way I figured it, the gorgeous wig would delight me and my date. I couldn't wait to flip my hair over my shoulder and watch him get shivers down his spine.

The big day finally arrived. I spent all afternoon preening and primping for the dance that would transform me into a sex kitten. When I finally placed my astonishing hair on my boring head, I was instantly transformed into a stunningly attractive woman—so dazzling that I hardly recognized myself in the mirror. I looked spectacular—like a starlet. Next up, I began practicing my flip. I tossed my head from side to side until I was an accomplished flipper. Wow, was I going to send shivers down male spines! The other guys at the dance will wish that they had asked me out. I was eager and ready for my first date to proceed. Nothing could have given me more self-confidence than that image-making mane. It was magic.

When my escort arrived at the front door and looked at me, he was a bit stunned. I saw his eyes instantaneously open wide like he'd seen a ghost. He probably thought for a second I was my sister or my mother! Suddenly I had long, light, shimmering hair. But I knew how to send him into a frenzy. He looked me in the eyes, and I peered back and flipped my hair. All I needed was a peacock feather in my mouth, but that would have been overkill. We excitedly headed for the dance.

I flipped my new hair all night long. I felt drop-dead gorgeous. Besides, I loved dancing, and he was a terrific dancer. So we spent hours on the dance floor making hot moves and celebrating my flip-flopping hair.

Toward the end of the evening, we started making some fancy ballroom dance moves and the other attendees began clearing off the dance floor to watch us. Pretty soon just the two of us were putting on a show for all the jealous gawkers. We were grooving. It was a splendid evening leading up to the very last dance, for which my fabulous partner and I decided to let loose. He was directing me like a great orchestra leader; we really synced. Then disaster struck.

He figured I could handle just about any dance move, so he decided to bend me back over his arm so far that I could practically reach back and touch the floor. After all, this was the kind of celebrated move that you might see in a movie or on television, not the lame sort of move you'd normally expect at a high school dance. It would truly put the rest of the dancers to shame. As he dropped me back like a limp towel over his arm, I immediately realized I had flipped my hair one too many times that evening. The wig slipped off my head and landed right in the middle of the dance floor for everyone to stare at. Thinking quickly, and nimble as a kitten, I reached down to grab it, but accidentally booted it like a hockey puck across the dance floor.

Even though we were a marvelous dance couple, he never asked me out again. I stored the wig in moth balls.

There's something captivating about becoming more than we already are. We all imagine becoming stronger, better looking, or more intelligent. We envision what we could become, not just what we are now. We're all dreamers. Whether we want to admit it or not, each of us knows down deep they we're not all that we could really be. We're intimate with our weaknesses and imperfections. Sometimes we fool others, but we still know our own flaws.

The combination of our dreams and our imperfections fuels much modern advertising, which is based on our innate desire to become more lovable. We're constantly told we need to have more lustrous hair, smoother skin, thinner or firmer bodies, more fashionable clothing, a hotter car, and so much more.

The women's magazines at supermarket checkout counters are the most amazing of all. If you're a man, here's your assignment: take a look at one of those magazines for four or five minutes, starting at the front cover. You'll be amazed that you might not even get to the table of contents for ten or twelve pages. The magazine will be chock-full of advertisements, nearly all of which tell women how they can attract men and successfully compete with other women. The cosmetic ads might seem a bit superficial, but women take them more or less to heart. Why? Partly because the stuff works! Guys do like sexier-looking women. Image matters. Also, women feel more self-confident when they look better in others' eyes.

In the end, though, temporary surface transformation doesn't really help people become deeply comfortable with themselves. We all know the whole system of makeup and fashion is largely phony—even if we play the game. External beauty is really cultural, not innate. After all, being plump is really sexy in some cultures. Who gets to define the best "image" in contemporary North American culture? Who gives them the authority? There's a lot of deception involved.

The Bible has some remarkable things to say about image-making. One of the most incredible verses about this is in the Old Testament, no less (the issue is hardly new). In 1 Samuel 16 we learn that the "Lord does not look at the things people look at. People look at the outward appearance, but the Lord looks at the heart" (7). We're all concerned with externals, whereas God puts his finger on the real deal, our most personal and private feelings about God, others, and ourselves. God looks at our hearts. Wigs, like make-up, can lie. The heart can't. It is what it is, even if we successfully conceal our hearts from others.

So the only really enduring transformation occurs in our hearts. That's where the love of God operates, too. God's not really interested in superficial updates to our external appearance beyond such essentials as modesty and appropriateness. He's interested in our whole-hearted transformation.

I'm overwhelmed by God's transforming power in my own life. I think of who I was before I truly knew him—a lonely, unattractive, self-loathing, insecure, confused, friend-less, unwanted young woman. My wig transformed me externally for one night—at least until I booted it across the slippery gym floor.

When I started loving Jesus Christ, however, he began transforming me into a member of a chosen people, a royal priesthood, and a holy nation. He began transforming my broken family relationships, and teaching me how to accept forgiveness and to forgive myself. He showed me how to laugh with others and not to take myself so seriously. He transformed my unknown, hazy future into a ministry with a heavenly purpose that fills my heart with meaning. My own transformation—and yours, too—comes down to what the apostle Paul proclaimed to the Galatians, "I have been crucified with Christ and I no longer live, but Christ lives in me. The life I live in the body, I live by faith in the Son of God, who loved me and gave himself for me" (2:20).

What in your life needs to be transformed? To begin with, your heart. If you haven't offered it to Jesus Christ, now is an ideal time. Do you need spiritual rejuvenation? An enriched marriage? Deeper friendships? Maybe you're dealing with unemployment or general financial difficulties. Perhaps you recently lost a loved one. Give all of your concerns to Jesus Christ.

Thank God for the gift of forgiveness and your resulting new life in Jesus Christ. Let the gratitude settle into your heart over time, day by day. Don't focus immediately on your own needs; focus on God's gift of Jesus Christ. This grace-centered living will begin changing your attitude toward yourself and your own life. Here's why: gratitude to God is the beginning of living faithfully in the world. When we start our day, job search, dating, or anything else with bitterness or despair, we almost guarantee failure and unhappiness. When we begin with gratitude, we become attentive to the opportunities God is unfolding all around us. After beginning each of your days and prayers with gratitude to God, then ask him for the wisdom and strength you'll need to make wise decisions as you move ahead faithfully.

Many Christian books about living faithfully and being successful are really self-help rather than God-help books. They implicitly assume what we ourselves *do* causes good or bad *results*. So they say "do this" and "do that" like a laundry list of ways to con God into getting what we want. Sometimes this kind of self-help stuff gets downright goofy, such as the warning that we should always end our prayers with a double "amen." These authors forget that the place to start is inner transformation, not outer efforts. We have to allow God to bathe us in gratitude so our hearts are filled with thankfulness. This kind of inner change begins transforming our lives into worship. Without such inner gratefulness, we invariably get frustrated that one or another self-help technique doesn't work.

Living faithfully out of gratitude to God will transform your life, even if not always in the ways you would expect. Get this: the writer of Hebrews says that Abraham, one of the great people of faith in the Old Testament, when "called to go to a place he would later receive as his inheritance, obeyed and went, even though he did not know where he was going" (11:8). True faith is never first of all about trying to get God to perform on our behalf. It's about trusting our loving God to do what's best for us even though we can't know in advance what the result will be. We can't trick God into giving us everything we want; trying to get God to give you exactly what you want is more like magic than faith.

Yet God truly wants us to ask for faith, wisdom, and peace. He wants us to ask him to show us the way toward a transformed life. You'll probably be surprised at how God answers your prayers, especially who he uses to model the faith and provide the insight you need to live obediently for him.

But just remember that our requests to God are a response to God's previous goodness toward us in the death and resurrection of Jesus Christ. God transforms us from the inside out as we worship him with thanksgiving, recognizing that every good thing flows from him. The Lord's Prayer itself begins with acknowledging that God is our hallowed, heavenly father—not with a declaration of our needs.

The greatest instruction manual for faithful living is the Bible. Together with other faithful followers of Jesus Christ, we learn about God and his will for our lives as we study and live out his Word together. Living in Christian community truly transforms us. To use the apostle Paul's language from his letter to the Romans, God wants us to be transformed by the "renewing" of our minds (12:2). When our hearts focus gratefully on loving God, our minds are free to learn how to live faithfully in every part of our lives, not just at church.

When we invite God to transform our hearts and our minds, we also learn new spiritual practices. We learn to trust his faithfulness, rest in his promises, and rely on his grace. We worship in spirit and truth rather than just because we have to go to church. We live openly from the heart, without phoniness. We set aside our spiritual wigs.

Instead of trying to be a superhero by leaping tall buildings in a single bound, or simply buying new hair to

Be Mine

send shivers, try thankfully accepting God's transforming love. Give yourself the space and time to participate in a celebrative Christian community. Let God's love fill in the empty holes of your life and change you into the new and improved version of yourself.

9

I Love You More Than You Can Wee

GOD'S LAVISH LOVE

Valentine's Day is a great time to lavish gifts on loved ones. Small and large tokens of affection make us smile, and gratify greeting card shops, florists, and candy companies. One of the best aspects of Valentine's Day is the excuse to express our love through thoughtful gifts and gentle words of appreciation. I'm blessed with a husband, David, who really has a talent for gift-giving. His presents are always meaningful expressions meant distinctly for me. The best gift he ever presented to me was a marriage proposal—the gift I accepted that has kept on giving. Since he first proposed, however, he's continued to delight me with wonderfully appropriate tokens of his love.

I love presenting special things to David, too. Unfortunately, I'm not very good at it. My lack of creativity coupled with my poor life skills generate some interesting surprises for him. One year I fervently sought to bake his favorite coconut cream pie. David was pleased with my effort, particularly because he knew I hated baking. But he wasn't so overjoyed when the meringue slipped off the pie, onto the floor, and settled in a blob resembling a diseased amoeba. I also once tried to bake brownies. When the baking period was over, I tested them; they seemed awfully gooey and underdone. So I tossed them back in the oven for another 10 minutes or so. Then they were really cooked. So was I. David had to chisel the brown bricks out of the pan and slice them with his diamond-bladed table saw.

After numerous kitchen disasters, I decided to write poetry to David. I discovered I'm a better poet than cook, although college students will never study my work except possibly in an anthropology class on graffiti. At least I'm able to compose meaningfully coherent thoughts and even some rhymes.

If only I were a better typist. My computer keyboarding is painfully slow and inaccurate; my fingers don't obey my brain, or vice versa. Everything I type requires careful editing, but I'm not a great proofer. Once I meant to type, "I love you more than you can see." It came out, "I love you more than you can wee." The verse sounded less romantic than I had hoped. Fortunately, I caught the error before I proudly presented the final draft to David. I can only imagine how he would have responded to my "wee" mistake. I think I'm safe now, given the age of his prostate.

My unintentionally creative typing is one of the reasons I left my part-time job as a church secretary. When I got my hands on church bulletins, anything could happen. I probably wrote half of the church bulletin bloopers postings found on the Internet—bloopers like "Evening massage at 6 p.m.," "a song fest was hell last week," and "for those who have children and don't know it, we have a nursery downstairs." All of those make sense to me on initial reading. Some of my mistakes are legendary and inappropriate for this book; nothing like a few naughty words to get the elders to give me special attention. I don't understand why software companies can't make spellcheckers that correct meaning as well as spelling. Now that would be a gift worth giving.

Nevertheless, I'm always searching for ingenious gift ideas. I especially like shopping for grandchildren. I would give them the world if I could, just to experience the enjoyment of watching their faces as they unwrap that present! With them, I don't even have to worry about misspelling my notes and cards.

God must really enjoy gift-giving. He did give us human beings the world to take care of and develop. Clearly he appreciates and accepts our meager, imperfect words and acts of gratitude toward him. Expressing gratitude is at the heart of worship and doesn't require perfection. Some of the apostle Paul's sentence prayers are so long that I couldn't ever figure out how to graph them into nouns, verbs, adjectives, adverbs, and whatever other literary devices the Holy Spirit employs through Paul.

How great are our needs for God's gifts!

My family experienced a time when the world seemed to be slamming us down so hard that we weren't sure we could ever rise again. David had just survived a life-threatening disease. Our son, Jeff, was recovering from being hit by a car while he was riding his bike. I had just been released from the hospital after a very serious bout of pancreatitis.

In the midst of all of these health issues, we discovered that a trusted business partner had absconded with all of the money and moved to Mexico, leaving us thousands of dollars in debt. We felt convicted that God wanted us to honor all of the debts and avoid bankruptcy. So we lived with the consequences; we eventually lost everything we owned, including our personal savings and our home. There were times when we didn't have enough food to eat and we lacked money to buy more. We didn't know how we were going to survive financially. We were deep in the pit.

But God wasn't going to leave us there. Gifts started pouring in. One day I had nothing left in the pantry except oatmeal, and someone left two bags of groceries on our doorstep. The next week a sweet widow from church sent us a check for $10—enough to get us through the week. All the way through our extremely difficult period, God was never late with gifts.

Sometimes we felt like we had nothing left but the gift of prayer. But even that seemed to be enough at critical times. We once went to our church elder's house to pray for God's guidance. When we returned, we picked up the mail on the way into the house. The envelopes included a letter from a college asking my husband if he was interested in a temporary appointment teaching college biology. God was at it again, calling on others to serve us.

In order to accept David's new job, we moved from sunny San Diego to snowy Grand Rapids, Michigan—in

January. We lacked coats let alone shovels. We had no idea what to expect. But God had gone before us, and we were warmly welcomed. It was almost like we had come home to a place we never resided. We managed to rent a small duplex near the college, content in the fact that we would probably never own a home again.

But God wasn't done lavishing gifts of grace upon us. We joined a wonderfully hospitable church and felt deeply loved. When an elder and deacon of the church came to our duplex to greet us, we told them the story of how we had come to town. It turned out the deacon was a multimillionaire (this is a good thing to try to arrange when you're broke and you join a church) who was truly passionate about serving God and helping others. He was so impressed that David and I had decided not to declare bankruptcy that several weeks later he called us to offer a $20,000 interest-free loan so we could buy a house. We were flabbergasted.

We purchased a lovely home near campus. Filled with gratitude, we dedicated it to God's service. Over the years we have sheltered numerous young people.

A few months later, the same self-sacrificial deacon called to say that God was leading him to cancel our debt. Suddenly we owed him nothing. We had plenty of needs, but it seemed like God was always there, addressing them before we could totally freak out.

Of course, economic and physical needs are never the end of the story for any of us. We all have psychological and emotional needs as well. We have spiritual needs, some-times even profound crises of faith. It's understandable that people are gripped by fear in tough times. People lose jobs and health care benefits. Some suffer foreclosed homes. Large corporations downsize and lay off scads of workers. College students pursue a major only to find out that they don't like it or it doesn't suit their gifts and talents—and they're suddenly unemployed after getting their degree. Relationships fall apart between spouses, and among children, extended families, and friends. Financial stresses create interpersonal conflicts. The future can appear incredibly bleak and daunting.

Amidst all of our worry, however, God offers his lavish love. Jesus says over and over again that we shouldn't fear; he knows what really grips us. He doesn't always give us exactly what we want. But when our hearts are open, we see his blessings even in the most taken-for- granted dimensions of everyday life. If we pay attention, God is all around us, pouring out his blessings with good and perfect gifts—just as he promised (James 1:17). The Bible is full of God's promises; scripture demonstrates his faithfulness in keeping his promises. The apostle Paul tells us in Philippians 4 that "God will meet all your needs according to the riches of his glory in Christ Jesus" (19). Paul also reminds us that "God is able to bless you abundantly, so that in all things at all times, having all that you need, you will abound in every good work" (2 Cor. 9:8).

Wherever you are on your life journey, whatever is hap-pening in your life, whatever your needs right now, take it all to your loving father in prayer. Sincerely ask for what you need. At the same time, connect with other Christians so you can love and serve one another as you together bring your needs to the Lord. We're created for community, which God frequently uses to meet our needs and give us joy. God longs to lavish his love upon you.

I've been blessed with two granddaughters. Imagine if they came to me and said, "Granny, please love me more." There's no way I would ever refuse them. God loves you more than I could ever love my granddaughters. And he won't ever refuse to love you.

We won't always give one another the perfect gift. We may not even agree on what the ideal gift is for each other! Good intentions help, but the execution is important, too. Your meringue might fall flat on the floor. But our father knows how to give perfect love, faultlessly. Whatever your emotional, physical, spiritual, relational, and financial needs, turn to him and to other believers. Give thanks together. Trust him. Rest in his love. It's always lavish and it's never too late.

10

Pull The Drapes
GOD'S DISCIPLINARY LOVE

*C*hildren can't comprehend how strenuous and tedious disciplining them can really be. Life would be so much easier if parents could just sit on the sofa and read a book all day without having to worry about raising their offspring. But because we love our children and don't want them to get into trouble, we dedicate a lot of time and energy to correcting them.

I recall seeing my three-year-old son, Jeff, riding his bike in the street. I called him into the house to remind him of our rule, "Thou shalt not ride thy bicycle in yonder street." I informed him once again that I expected him to observe that simple rule—and that I had better not see him riding in the street again. I thought I was mighty persuasive. But he looked at me with his innocent blue eyes and responded, "Pull the drapes." He had a point. It was a funny line even if it was a lousy solution to his problem, and hardly an approach that would eliminate my fears.

Be Mine

Our heavenly father loves us just as we are, but he also understands the importance of disciplining us and showing us how to discipline ourselves. Most of us have areas in life where we struggle to be obedient, such as the secret sins we enjoy and don't want to give up for Lent or anything else.

For me, the biggest issue is food. I love munchies. But I love food too much, and I love too much food. That's why I'm a bit fluffy (a.k.a. fat).

Skinny people have always been an enigma to me. Why do they actually prefer a small salad with diet dressing on the side to a gloriously greasy order of cheesy fries sprinkled generously with salt and smothered in ketchup (I'm salivating like Pavlov's dogs as I write this)? How can scrawny folks push lettuce leaves around their plate, eat only half of their rabbit food, and then declare themselves full? And how are they able to pull that off in the same amount of time it takes me to down a cheeseburger and order a chocolate dessert? I just don't get it.

More than that, I don't comprehend how anyone can "forget to eat." To me, eating is like breathing. I never forget it. In fact, chowing down is one of the few things I effortlessly remember. Not only that, I'm never too tired to eat. I'm never too stressed, busy, sick, or anything else to snarf down a snack. I eat in my dreams. I'm a culinary multi-tasker; I can eat cookies, drive the car, listen to the radio, drink a soda, and daydream about chocolate all at the same time. When it comes to food, I have one major comment: "Bring it on, baby!"

In addition to enjoying just about any vittles, I'm blessed with slow metabolism and short stature. I'm gravitationally depressed and calorically gifted. So along with being chronologically mature, I can say I'm old, short, and fluffy. I've prayed to be taller and to acquire the metabolism of an Olympic athlete. I even told God I'm not fussy; I'd accept either one. Unfortunately, he seems to have a different option in mind for me—that bothersome option called "self control."

I've been on and off weight-loss diets my whole life. I've lost probably 3,000-4,000 pounds over the years, only to regain them in the same prime locations.

A while back my husband and I even dieted together—what true love! He had developed a little professorial bulge and accompanying love handles on his own way to becoming fluffy. With feigned humility and a little exaggeration, I'd say I'm a near-perfect wife even when we're under the stress of duo-dieting. I tried daily to offer David at least one uplifting comment. So after we had been dieting for a few weeks, I said to him one morning, "Honey, I think you're starting to look a little thinner." He turned, peered directly at me, and instantly replied, "I wish I could say the same thing for you." That wasn't the world's highest praise, but I immediately returned the compliment. I looked into his eyes and proclaimed, "Well, you could if you lied like I do!" So goes marital repartee during a diet phase.

Fighting my obsession with food is a constant, grueling battle, so I look for ways out. Sometimes I wonder if gluttony really is a sin. Where does the Bible actually say that growing a spare tire is morally wrong? What about Abel? He brought to the Lord fat portions from some of the firstborn of his flock, not from his own tummy. And the Lord was pleased (Gen. 4:4). Then again, Proverbs 23 is really a dieter's downer. Ponder this: "When you sit to dine with a ruler, note well what is before you, and put a knife to your throat if you are given to gluttony" (1-2). Well, so far no ruler has invited me to dine, so I guess my throat is safe for now.

Seriously, it's so easy to rationalize our obsessions. No matter how I try to sugarcoat it, my overeating is an act of disobedience to God. Like other favorite sins, it's extraordinarily difficult to give up. This kind of gripping obsession can become so established in our lives that we're no longer able to identify it as disobedience. Most of the time, however, I think we realize that such obsessions—or even addictions—don't jibe with God's will. That's why we don't usually flaunt them; we pretend to be attending to them while trying to participate in them more moderately.

We might hope that God would always intervene directly to wipe out our immoderate desires. In my experience, however, this isn't normally the way our heavenly father operates. Instead, it seems to me, God uses the natural consequences of our disobedience to get our attention. He lets us discover the depth of our trouble so we might honestly ponder how we got into the mess and how we can get out of it. Remember that God's beloved children, Israel, chose to continue to disobey and worship other gods, to treat each other unjustly, and basically to defy God's law. God didn't fix everything for them overnight. He let them suffer the consequences of their waywardness. They were captured and taken into captivity. God never abandoned them and never stopped loving them. Nevertheless, he let their predicament stand as evidence for their disobedience.

God knows what it would be like for us to choose life over death in every part of our lives. He wants us to choose life and to give up those things that are bad for ourselves and others. Yet there's something about us having to make and live with choices that's part of the way God loves us. He understands the importance of discipline and especially self-discipline in our sanctification. It's not that God goes around creating painful situations in order to bring us to distress and induce fear in our hearts. I don't think God desires to punish us per se. It's just that he needs to discipline us for our own good so we make right and fitting choices from our hearts.

Maybe it helps to consider the difference between punishment and discipline. Punishment is an end in itself that teaches a lesson through deprivation or retribution. Punishment often involves creating physical, emotional, or social pain for the person being punished. God's discipline is different than mere punishment; his discipline is really meant to help people grow, develop, and shuck anything that might be keeping them in bondage. God wants us to be free to achieve our greatest potential as faithful followers of Jesus Christ. He wants to nurture our faithfulness both as individuals and in Christian community. After praising God for his great mercy and for Jesus' resurrection, Peter writes," In all this you greatly rejoice, though now for a little while you may have had to suffer grief in all kinds of trials. These have come so that the proven genuineness of your faith—of greater worth than gold, which perishes even though refined by fire—may result in praise, glory and honor when Jesus Christ is revealed" (1 Pet. 1:6-7).

Your faith, your well-being, and your relationship with God are of utmost importance to him. He will do his part to enable you to be the person he created you to be. He loves you too much to respond otherwise.

Discipline is one way God forms us into holier people. Referring to Proverbs, the writer of Hebrews says, "'My son, do not make light of the Lord's discipline, and do not lose heart when he rebukes you, because the Lord disciplines the one he loves, and he chastens everyone he accepts as his son.' Endure hardship as discipline; God is treating you as his children. For what children are not disciplined by their father?" (12:4-7).

Most of us experience difficult situations that tempt us to lash out at God. In some of these situations, such as the loss of a loved one, angry lament might be the most honest response to what has occurred. We naturally cry out to God, "Why would you let this happen?"

In less catastrophic situations, it's too easy to blame God for our or others' disobedience. When we do things that cause physical or emotional harm, we need to fess up. In such cases we should withhold some of our immediate anger or frustration and consider asking God a far different question, "What do you want me to learn from this?" We can also ask God to show us if there is anything in our lives or even our deep past that's causing us to act selfishly or obsessively. After asking such questions, it makes sense to give ourselves time to listen to God and others, and even to our own hearts.

No one likes to be disciplined. Children sometimes appreciate discipline after the fact because it gives them direction and sets limits as they try to please their parents. Even for adults, suffering is a different story. We adults don't like to suffer. We prefer not to struggle. We'd like to avoid pain and despair. We would prefer to conduct our lives on the mountaintops rather than in the valleys.

Ironically, there isn't much vegetation at the apex of real mountains. There's just a lot of barren land and rocks. Lush, nourishing plants flourish in the valleys. To some extent, the valleys of life most discipline us to choose life over death. We just need to try to remember along the way that God climbs over the mountains and walks through the valleys with us. He promises never to leave or forsake us (Heb. 13:5). Even if we turn our backs on God, he won't abandon us.

Think back to a time when you were lovingly disciplined by your parents. At the time, the parental discipline probably didn't feel very good. You might also recall when you recognized your own disobedience, apologized, and learned from your former way. Most likely your parents embraced you even more lovingly in return. Remember the joy of hearing them say, "I forgive you." Remember, too, the feeling of freedom and renewal you felt when the discipline was over. That's somewhat like learning from God, ceasing to disobey him, offering him our apologies, and moving ahead in faith. Such discipline is one of the great ways our

Lord teaches us how to love. Let his loving arms of grace envelope you so you feel the freedom of restoration and the hope of renewal. Then remember not to ride your bicycle into the street again.

11

Hey, Little Girl
GOD'S SANCTUARY LOVE

O ne Sunday morning my husband, David, and I were at church. We had already attended the first morning service and for some reason were planning to attend the second one as well. Chatting with our friends between services, I privately said to David, "I've got to pee!" Not liking to draw attention to himself when we entered the sanctuary for worship, he replied "Well, get in there and go because I don't want to parade down front for the next service."

David's comment reflects one of the basic differences between the two of us. I love attention. I love sitting in the front of church where others can see me. I like to be so close to the front that I can discern whether or not our minister successfully trimmed his nose hairs the previous night. And I love "working the crowd" as I parade down the aisle toward the front before each service, greeting friends and offering friendly waves. But I'm generally an easy-going and semi-flexible spouse, too, so I said to David, only a little bit snarkily, "Yes, sir." I dashed to the restroom and completed my task expediently, especially considering all of the different layers, buttons, belts, and zippers I had to contend with, all the way down to my feisty pantyhose.

I soon rejoined David and our friends to continue the discussion as if I'd never left. Then I noticed a strange breeze coming through the narthex, as if someone had left open a door. Moreover, people passing behind me seemed to be breaking out in smiles and chuckles. I thought to myself, "What a cheerful and sociable congregation!" After about five minutes, I realized I had to scratch an itch on my lower back. I reached around back to scratch it and discovered a major embarrassment.

Apparently when I had pulled up my pantyhose in the bathroom the hem of my skirt got caught in the waistband. Since returning from the restroom and chatting with our friends in the narthex, I had been inadvertently mooning about half of the congregation—and no one had said anything to me as they pondered my scantily clad rear end. No wonder everybody was giggling! No wonder it felt so breezy and cheery in the narthex. I ran to every woman's refuge—the bathroom, or restroom as the elite call it. Moreover, I hid there until after the service began. For the first time in memory, I didn't parade down front before worshiping God.

Embarrassing incidents usually cause me to want to run away and hide. I'm convinced no one likes to face the people who just witnessed their own embarrassing actions. We need a safe place to regroup, a sanctuary where we will not be judged and where we can bear our souls rather than our fannies. The bathroom worked temporarily for me in this case. But what about serious embarrassments? What about shameful situations where we offend others or really do something awful that we hate for anyone to know about? Only after spending time in God's sanctuary are we then able to face the world anew.

Sometimes we simply have to seek out the kind of refuge that allows us to address openly the deepest of emotional and spiritual issues in our lives. These might include situations that truly crush our spirits; these can even be overwhelmingly frightening and emotionally raw circumstances. When they strike us, we long for peace and safety. We need the kind of safe haven we have in our relationship with God. We can always run to him and find the peace and understanding we need.

Once I was on a prayer retreat with my soul sister and accountability partner, Necia. During one of our prayer times together, I was confronted with a childhood memory I had buried for decades. In my recollections, I was about five or six years old on a Saturday evening. My parents were going out dancing and had hired a female babysitter to take care of my brothers and me.

Shortly after my parents departed, however, the babysitter called a couple of her male friends and invited them over to our house. After they arrived I could smell alcohol and was pretty sure they were drunk.

These unwelcome visitors started saying things to me I really didn't understand and made me feel dirty and uncomfortable inside: "Hey, little girl, you want to become a woman tonight?" "You want us to teach you what a really good time feels like?" I felt so disturbed and uncomfortable that I ran to my parents' bedroom because it was the only room with a lock. I locked myself inside and took shelter in the farthest corner from the door, rolled up in the fetal position, and crying. I was so scared that I was shaking. I felt alone, unprotected, and vulnerable.

Then these two guys began pounding on the door. They were laughing and yelling at me to come out so they could show me things I didn't understand. The room provided some safety, but I remember crying out, "Where's my mommy and daddy? Why won't they protect me?" Fortunately, the men never entered the room. I don't recall exactly when I came out, but I do remember that the babysitter made me agree not to tell my parents what had happened. So I buried the memory until decades later at the prayer retreat.

I shared this awful memory with Necia, who suggested I ask Jesus to show me where he was while this was happening. I had no idea where this kind of prayer was going, but I earnestly closed my eyes and asked God to answer the request.

The awful memory returned, but this time I could see Jesus kneeling beside me. His arms were spread out protectively like wings, enfolding and protecting me in his love. But most amazing were his tears. He was sobbing because his little girl, me, was not being taken care of and was hurting so badly. This new memory of Jesus caring earnestly about me has become precious because when I was a young child I didn't know Jesus Christ. Of course, he knew I would one day be part of his family even as he kept me safe from the two men who were banging on the door and making me feel so awful. He did protect me, even though I didn't know it at the time.

Jesus is an always-available sanctuary. When you feel the need for a refuge from feeling attacked or abandoned, or from circumstances driving you away from those who exploit or abuse you, remember that Jesus is there with you.

Jesus seeks our healing, not our embarrassment or judgment. Sometimes we need a refuge because of uncontrollable events such as death and disease. Other times we face horrible disappointments such as broken relationships and unfaithful friends and relatives. Yet other times we're embarrassed because of what others wrongly did to us. Life can become so stormy that our hearts turn raw and hurting. We then need an asylum where we can discover healing.

I can't answer the question as to why God allows evil to happen to us. Why did the Lord permit the babysitter to invite those two adolescent thugs to my home? Why did Jesus permit me to go through such a traumatizing circumstance? I just don't know. All I can say is that in this deeply broken world where the devil still operates, however limited, we all experience emotionally wrenching and faith-challenging events. The devil hopes we will be overcome with fear and doubt. God wants us to experience his love through healing. As the world around us quakes with violence and injustice, we need God's loving arms to embrace us without fearing that Jesus will reject us. My life experiences have taught me that God's presence can be a kind of safe sanctuary to help us in our emotional, physical, and spiritual struggles.

Our problem is that we can too easily blame ourselves for others' cruelty. We focus on our embarrassment or regret rather than on others' inappropriate or even evil ways. For instance, women frequently suffer horrible abuse and then wrongly blame themselves as if they had caused it. When that babysitter made me promise not to tell my parents about what had happened, she was contributing to my own sense of responsibility for what occurred—or at least to my sense that I would be responsible for any negative repercussions for her and her buddies. She took advantage of me rather than honestly facing her own misdeeds and apologizing to my parents, brothers, and me. Children are especially vulnerable to such adult irresponsibility. And they're quick to think they caused the way they were treated.

If you're at a place in your life where you feel the need for refuge, turn to the book of Psalms. Let the poetic words create an image of God's open arms. "Hide me in the shadow of your wings," says the psalmist (17:8). "The Lord is my rock, my fortress and my deliverer; my God is my rock, in whom I take refuge" (18:2). "He is our help and our shield" (33:20). "Be my rock of refuge, to which I can always go; give the command to save me, for you are my rock and my fortress" (71:3). Using psalmic imagery, Jesus calls us his "chicks" and says he seeks to gather us together under his wings (Matt. 23:37). Reading such words quiets my heart and helps me to feel enfolded in God's love. It also gives me the courage to speak to others about my experiences.

Let such words and images wash over you like gentle waves of grace. Be refreshed and assured that no matter what you're going through, God's love is there to protect, strengthen, and ultimately deliver you. He longs to be your refuge. He yearns to be your sanctuary. Turn to him in your distress and you will find rest and restoration.

Moreover, the presence of Jesus comes to us through the unconditional love of others who find sanctuary in him, too. Necia helped me find Jesus' love in the midst of my horrible memories. She and other brothers and sisters in Christ have served me with their time, energy, and wisdom so I might more fully experience God's sanctuary love.

Being embarrassed is a part of life. So is wrongly feeling ashamed for others' misdeeds. People will make fun of us, just as we sometimes make fun of others. Some people will even intentionally hurt and exploit us. We do need a safe place to recover, but we also need safe friends and family who will dwell in God's sanctuary with us. The psalmist and Jesus remind us we are never alone—even when our loved ones and others responsible for us let us down. God is present, always listening, constantly comforting. He seeks justice as well as love.

Thanks to my friend, Necia, and her patient love for me, I was able to find peace decades after the original event that so traumatized me as a child. Today I especially appreciate the picture of running to God with my broken heart and having him scoop me up in his arms and hold me close to his chest as he rocks me back and forth, gently assuring me that all will be fine. In his love and community, we all rediscover God's loving sanctuary—even after unintentionally mooning our brothers and sisters in Christ.

12

Turkeys Bigger than Her Bodice

GOD'S UPLIFTING LOVE

I'm repeatedly amazed that so many people actually like to shop. All I can say to them is, "Why?" In my admittedly uncommon view, shopping is an annoying, exhausting, and frustrating activity that requires me to part with my hard-earned cash. For me, shopping is truly an exceptional event because I go shopping only as an alternative to doing almost anything else. Don't expect to see me in a shopping mall, except perhaps in the food court.

In fact, I vividly recall the last time I went mall shopping by myself—and I'm not talking last month or even last year. I had lost a wealth of weight—which later reappeared—and really felt good about myself. More than that, I truly looked good. Really good. I was looking so fine that I decided to reward myself with something potentially even more sensual than a cheeseburger and fries. Thinking of my husband as well as myself, I concluded it was a fitting time to take the mall by storm in order to buy a long, slinky nightgown. I was not "going shopping" as much as going to buy a particular item in a particular mall. I could handle that—I thought.

Because I hate to go shopping and I don't like spending money, I normally purchase items at one of the large, free-standing, super-discount venues that stocks just about everything except automobiles. If they don't sell something, I figure it's not worth owning. They do peddle women's lingerie, but this time I was on mission to locate the kind of high-end attire you wouldn't find displayed under the big-box stores' fluorescent lights and on their cheap racks scattered around their tasteless cement floors.

I didn't want other random shoppers watching me sift through racks of revealing undergarments and hold each skimpy item up to my body to see if I could squeeze into it. I certainly didn't want to put the slinky item in a cart for the checkout clerk to bag with my golden bananas. I wanted to purchase this ultra-important item at a store that would privately place the nightgown in a fancy store bag with an impressive logo on it, not just squish it in the same kind of cheap plastic bags I use to line my small trash cans at home. After all, I was going to put this piece of clothing on my naked body. I didn't want to have to first wash out the banana smell for fear it might not survive even one cleaning before turning into a stringy mess of torn lace and stained silk. Neither bananas nor stringy lace turn on my husband—to the best of my knowledge.

A personal mission doesn't always guarantee courage, however, and I had plenty of fear about shopping at the mall for something so classy. Just the thought of going to the mall strikes terror in my heart and causes me to break out in hives. Now I was actually thinking about hitting the mall to shop for something very intimate and personal. I guess I suffered from temporary insanity. To me, the mall is a place of torture rather than relaxation. In this case, though, I was resolute in my desire to treat my new, slimmed-down self to an elegant, right-fitting, super-silky, drop-dead-sexy nightgown. Why? Because I was absolutely convinced I deserved it.

There's nothing like losing weight to make me feel good about myself. I deserved this nightgown so much I wasn't even going to shop at the larger department stores located on the ends of the mall for easy access. I was going to enter the consumer holy of holies somewhere along one of the main aisles lined with those dinky shops with French names, hot lighting, and mannequins that look like emaciated extraterrestrials.

I summoned all of my courage, entered the mall, and checked my arms for hives. So far, so good. I proceeded to scout out the appropriate store. In no time flat I found a lingerie shop and confidently strolled through the door and into the sensual reddish lighting. I was on a roll.

As the angelic sales clerk approached me, however, I realized I might be in a bit of trouble. She was thin. Excruciatingly thin. Surely she never ate cheeseburgers. She must live a dull life, I rationalized to myself, not wanting to consider for a moment that even with my weight loss I wasn't in the same body league with her. I got nervous because I figured she couldn't possibly empathize with a fuller-figured and better-fed woman such as myself. Heck,

I had cooked Thanksgiving turkeys bigger than her bodice. Nevertheless, I decided not to let her diminutive figure deter me from accomplishing my lofty goal.

So I explained to the slim young thing that I was looking to purchase a nightgown with my hard-earned plastic. She looked me up and down, apparently trying to discern my official size. Then she began searching all around the store as if she couldn't locate anything that would fit even my slimmed-down body. I could almost hear her thoughts, "Why didn't I take an early lunch so I wouldn't have to deal with this clueless customer with the rhino carcass." Her body told me this when she tossed her hips from side to side with every provocative step she took around the chrome store racks. Finally, she suggested that she might have something in the back room that would fit me. Undaunted, I politely suggested that she take a look behind the magic curtain.

The model sales clerk returned holding out a gorgeous nightgown that probably weighed two ounces and would set me back $200. I eyeballed it, looked at her, perused my body, and made a wise decision. There was no way I was going to purchase that skimpy little thing from that skinny little thing. I managed to thank her for her trouble and explained that as lovely as the nightgown was I just thought it wouldn't quite work for me. I didn't inform her the last time I'd seen anything that slim it had only a tiny amount of toothpaste left in it.

I self confidently left the lingerie shop, migrated down the hallway, and consoled myself with a bag of just-baked, super-gooey, gloriously fattening, heavenly unhealthy, white chocolate chip and macadamia nut cookies. And I didn't share them with anyone. I deserved each and every one of those sultry sweets. I had been impressively daring, proving that I could tackle nearly any task set before me by friend or foe.

I think it's essential to celebrate ourselves each day. Not to celebrate ourselves for the sake of ourselves, but to thank God for giving us life. It helps us keep a healthy, emotional balance between tolerating ourselves and flaunting ourselves.

Part of being human is a powerful need to feel that we have worth and significance. In a perfect world, we would all be surrounded by others' affirmations of our worth from the moment we are born. This would continue through childhood and our adult years. But the fact is that far too many of us have never been deeply affirmed as God's valuable children. Often parents spend so much time dealing with their own insecurities and poor self-esteem that they don't have time or know-how when it comes to raising well-adjusted children of God. Moreover, some classmates and teachers inadvertently strip away students' self-confidence. Even friends and loved ones can unintentionally make us feel worthless by endlessly criticizing us and failing to express love, encouragement, and support.

I know, because I've struggled with feelings of worthlessness all my life. I accept the fact that my mother and father did their best to love me and to be good parents. Nevertheless, as a child I didn't feel loved. I always felt left out—like I was the one on the outside looking in at other peoples' fun and joy. It seemed to me, although I could be wrong, that my parents lavished their attention on my younger brothers. I felt like a worthless, ugly, scrawny kid. I longed to be coddled. At times I was so desperate for physical touch I would pretend to be sick so someone would take my temperature or rub special ointment on my chest.

Almost every night, I was reminded that I wasn't worth touching. The bedtime ritual at my house included a chasing game. The rules were simple. All three of us kids would try to run up the narrow stairway to the second floor, pushing and shoving to get to the top before dad caught us. If he snagged one of us, he tickled us mercilessly (or so we pretended). We tried to pretend we didn't want to get caught, but we all knew the most fun was to be the one he grabbed and tickled. I never got caught even though I wasn't always the fastest climber.

I was about nineteen years old when I finally found the type of affirmation I longed for. I then came to know Jesus Christ. I learned that because of his sacrifice I was—and am—a person of great worth. I discovered not only that God created me in his image and likeness, but also that everyone who follows Jesus Christ is a beloved child of God with a unique place in God's family. I began understanding that my worth doesn't depend on how well I perform in life or which people like me.

Now I empathize with others who similarly grew up without a sense of their inestimable value in God's eyes. Do you struggle with feelings of unworthiness? Do you long for assurance that your life has significance? Have you been crushed by unkind words or lies that have been spoken into your life—perhaps even lies about your value in God's eyes?

I'm amazed at the various ways people try to find affirmation. Many waste much of their time, energy, and money pursuing empty activities and ideals, only to discover that these things leave them emptier than before. Both men and women naively believe that physical beauty is proof of their worth. Advertisers count on our desire to become attractive by buying and flaunting products peddled on the basis of making us feel more attractive, successful, powerful, and smart. There's nothing wrong with wanting to look or feel good about ourselves, but we can't simply purchase meaningful self-esteem; consumerism is a bottomless pit of temporary satisfactions, an endless string of ultimately insufficient purchases.

The old adage that "beauty is only skin deep" is telling. Someone may look striking on the outside but feel unattractive on the inside. Good looks don't guarantee interpersonal skills or soulmates.

Countless people feel that wealth is a sure way of winning friends, so they amass a healthy financial portfolio and impress others with their lavish lifestyle. Yet some of the most insecure and unhappy people I've ever met base their sense of worth solely on their riches; they can have a lot of acquaintances who appreciate their largess, but they might not have many close friends who will stay with them through thick and thin. Others find that intelligence and advanced college degrees give them status as prominent members of their communities, but do little for their family life.

The result of such outward beauty and inner turmoil is a lifetime of regrets. Not until their life on earth is nearly over do they realize how few meaningful relationships they had. Too often, they die lonely and unloved, not just because they were wealthy or socially esteemed, but because their inner life was so strained that they ended up living in superficial relationships with God and others.

Sometimes I have an opportunity to share the good news with successful but forlorn people. I read to them the same scripture I read to myself to reassure me of my significance in God's world. Shortly after I became a Christian, I discovered 1 Corinthians 6:19-20, which powerfully reminds us that even our bodies are not our own (we belong to God), because we were bought with a price (the cross), and that we should honor God with our body (not just with our hearts and minds). In other words, God's love for us is all-encompassing, and we should respond gratefully with our entire selves.

The first part of Paul's words to the Corinthian church reminds us we are not our own. We belong fully to Jesus Christ. How great is that! We no longer have to suffer excessive loneliness or feelings of abandonment—only to accept God's assurance of us personally being chosen and used in his service.

Let's face it, the sovereign God of the universe doesn't really need us. He wants us. He wants you. God's desire for fellowship with us demonstrates our importance to him.

We are members of his family, chosen and adopted by him. We belong. That's a reason to celebrate. I say bring on the cake and ice cream. Let the streamers flow and noisemakers sound. We are God's beloved!

Next we see in this scripture that we were bought with a price—an extremely high price, namely, God's sacrifice of his own son. That purchase price proves beyond a shadow of a doubt that both you and I are people of extravagant worth. While writing this section of the book, I was so overcome with humbling gratitude for the depth of God's love for me that I had to stop, get on my knees, and thank him.

If you've never really meditated on God's momentous gift to us, you might stop reading and do likewise. Let the scope of God's love permeate your mind and heart. God's love for us is so vast that he paid the ultimate price for our salvation. We can't fully comprehend this, but we certainly can worship the God who has accomplished such a marvelous gift on our behalf.

What was it like for God to watch his only son be rejected, mocked, beaten, tortured, and ultimately crucified? I attempt to imagine how I would feel if I had to watch my child being treated like that. I would try to intervene, to save my child from such a horrific death on a cross. As humans, we don't always have the power to save our children, but God did have the authority. He could have stopped Jesus' crucifixion at any time, yet he didn't. Why? Because he knew you would be born one day, and he wanted you as his child forever. That feat required a savior to pay for your sins. So God was willing to watch as all the sins of humanity were placed on his only son. Then, because God cannot associate with sin, he had to turn away from his son. How dare we say we don't have worth! Christ's sacrifice proves that we do.

To further show we're people of worth, the last part of this section of Paul's letter to the Corinthians reminds us that God has chosen us not only to bear his image, but also to bring him glory. Would the all-knowing Creator of the universe choose a worthless person to carry out that critical task? Of course not.

Every morning I ask God to open my eyes to opportunities to bring him glory by being a blessing to someone that day. Each new day becomes an adventure because I never know how God is going to use me to serve others. What a joyous and exciting way to go through life. You might consider beginning your day with a similar prayer. It will help you thank God during the rest of the day and will make you more attentive to the good works God will be doing through you.

You might totally enjoy shopping and seeking bargains or even just hanging out at the mall. Good for you. Or you might share my dislike of the mall experience. Either way, you know that no one likes paying real money for a worthless product even if it's on sale. Because God loves us so much, he chose to pay the ultimate price for us. He bought our salvation through the death and resurrection of his only son. He loved us royally—and still does. Accept his love. Thank him for it. Celebrate God's love every day by bringing him glory and looking for ways to be a blessing to someone else—perhaps even at a hot lingerie shop.

13

Hair on the Chin
GOD'S ETERNAL LOVE

When we're young, we naively assume that many temporary things will last forever. Take our firm, young bodies as an example. A teenager might look at their mother's or father's body and think, "I'll never look like that." But decades of gravity and aging produce sagging, often flabby skin. The transformation is so pervasive that once a woman hits fifty she hesitates to raise her arm to wave goodbye, for fear she might be mistaken for a flying bat in drag, thanks to the dangling skin on her upper arms. A man hesitates to stand sideways in a photo for fear of looking pregnant. Oh, the joys of physical decline!

No one escapes such developments in spite of what advertisements portray. I get a good chuckle out of commercials for skin care products that promise to firm up and smooth out a woman's aging skin. Of course the depicted model is in her twenties, single, and works out daily with a professional trainer in her home gym. If we had stopped aging, we might look like her—depending on our own genetics. And how come the beefy hunks in beer commercials never suffer beer bellies?

I've been told that you can tell how old a woman is by the elasticity in the skin on the top of her hand. If you softly pinch and pull up the skin on the hand of a twenty-something, it will snap right back faster than you can see it happen. If you do the same thing on a fifty-year-old, it slowly oozes back into shape in a few minutes. If you try it with an eighty-year-old person, that skin will stay up there until Jesus returns. There's no way to get it snapping or oozing back without some outside help, like a skilled masseuse or special skin moisturizer. Even then, the results are temporary.

Of course, one should be happy that some things don't last forever. Take shaving legs, for instance. One of the benefits of females getting older is that the growth of leg hair diminishes greatly. Miracle of miracles, you don't have to shave your legs every day—or even once a week during winter if you live in the North. Pity the poor man whose hair growth increases in his ears and his nose while he loses it on top of his head. The bad news for women is that all the hair that used to grow on legs eventually populates the chin. At a certain age, women begin spending more time with tweezers than they ever did with shavers. Maybe it all evens out in the end—a little more hair here, a bit less there, until we just don't give a rip!

My point is that many, if not most, things do not last forever. The most sobering one is life. Our parents pass away. Eventually we pass away. So it goes.

One thing that does last forever, however, is God's faithfulness to all generations. We've all been disappointed by other people—including those we loved and trusted—who failed to return our love. They crushed our hearts, drained our joy, and made us fear new relationships. But God's love for us never really fades even if we're having trouble experiencing it.

I was in my late thirties when we moved from fast-growing San Diego to stable Grand Rapids, Michigan, where families had lived for generations. Many of these native Midwesterners had lived in the same communities from the time they were born. Most really didn't need a new outsider-friend like me. But I was desperate for just one female friend—a soul sister.

I prayed for several years in hopes of finding such a friend. During that time, I met many wonderful people, but no one so special that we could easily become deep and abiding friends. I had plenty of acquaintances, but not a truly kindred spirit. I longed to find one.

Finally, it happened. There she was—just as wacky and noisy as me. Her personality was also bigger than life, and she loved to laugh—at both herself and life. Best of all, she loved Jesus Christ with the same passion I did. It didn't take long for us to become best friends.

Then something devastating happened. For some inexplicable reason—still unknown to me—she stopped talking to me. That was it. The end. She wouldn't even take my calls. On top of that, she began spreading unkind words about me. I felt like my whole world had crumbled around me. Where could I go to feel accepted and validated again? With whom could I share my private thoughts without fear?

I needed a new friend. I wasn't yet trusting enough to jump into the search for a replacement for the one I had inexplicably lost. I needed time. I needed healing. I needed to reconnect with the only John 15 friend who had sacrificed his life for me and would forever remain true to me in spite of my weaknesses, insecurities, and uncertainties. I discovered that God was there with me, all along. God was already beside me as my faithful father, my Lord, my Creator, my provider, my sustainer, and my truest friend.

Who has let you down? Has it been parents, other family members, perhaps children, fellow church members, co-workers, or a best friend? I encourage you to do what I finally learned to do—to make God the number one relationship in your life. His love is constant, forever, and true. I cherish the words of Psalm 27:10: "Though my father and mother forsake me, the Lord will receive me." I treasure the magnificent promise of Deuteronomy 31:6, "Be strong and courageous. Do not be afraid or terrified because of [enemies], for the Lord your God goes with you; he will never leave you nor forsake you." Now that's a guarantee you can count on! You need not fear or doubt; be assured that God's love will last forever.

God's love is not just for this lifetime, but for all eternity. He invites us to everlasting, blessed fellowship. As wonderful as his love is here and now, we can be assured that it will be even greater when we see him face-to-face. The apostle Paul writes to the church at Corinth that what we experience in this life is "only a reflection as in a mirror" of things to come (1 Cor 13:12). Eventually all veils and barriers will be removed, and we will experience an intimate love we can't fully fathom. I long for that day even as I relish today. The blessings of today are a foretaste of the new earth God is unfolding through grace. I pray you will be with me in our father's presence, celebrating your finest friend's divine valentine for eternity.